APUSH Pocket Dictionary

*A Concise Reference
for the AP U.S. History Exam*

APUSH Pocket Dictionary: A Concise Reference for the AP U.S. History Exam

OTHER BOOKS IN THE STAMPEDE LEARNING SERIES:

AP U.S. History Exam Prep Guide and Course Reader: Master the Most Critical Content in a Hurry

APUSH Writing Guide: How to Write Winning Responses to DBQs, LEQs, and SAQs on the AP U.S. History Exam

Stampede Learning Systems
PO Box 44273
Milwaukee, Wisconsin 53214
www.StampedeLearning.com
info@StampedeLearning.com

ISBN: 978-0-9992794-1-0

First Edition: February 2018

10 9 8 7 6 5 4

CONTENTS

Introduction

TO SUCCEED ON THE AP U.S. HISTORY EXAM, it is essential that you master an understanding of the important people, events, and concepts that make up America's rich and complicated history.

This guide provides concise definitions of hundreds of key terms, including their historical significance and, when applicable, cause-and-effect relationships between them. Knowing this information will help you perform well on the Multiple Choice section of the AP exam, which makes up approximately 40% of your exam score. It will also arm you with facts that you can use as evidence when writing your responses to the Short Answer Question (SAQ), Long Essay Question (LEQ), and Document-Based Question (DBQ) portions of the exam.

You can use this book as a reference companion to the textbook assigned by your teacher. It is also the perfect accompaniment to our own book, *AP U.S. History Exam Prep Guide and Course Reader: A Stampede Learning Guide*. When reading your history text or working through exercises in our study guide, if you need a refresher on the significance of a person, issue, or event, look it up here and find the information you need, fast.

As you study for tests and write essays throughout the year, check out the relevant entries in this book to help you prepare. And of course, you can use this book to quiz yourself as you study for the AP exam. We wish you luck in your course and on the APUSH exam!

Dictionary
of Key U.S. History Terms

10% Plan	Part of President Lincoln's Reconstruction plan; required 10% of a Confederate state's population to swear loyalty to the Union.
13th Amendment	Abolished slavery.
14th Amendment	Granted freedmen the same rights as all other Americans; ensured they were protected by the Bill of Rights and the Constitution.
15th Amendment	Gave freedmen the right to vote.
16th Street Baptist Church Bombing	Four members of the KKK detonated a bomb at an African-American church in Birmingham, Alabama in 1963. The explosion killed four young girls and injured 22. This act of terrorism contributed to the passage of the Civil Rights Act of 1964.
17th Parallel	Served as the border between North Vietnam (which was communist) and South Vietnam (which was not) during the Vietnam War.
18th Amendment	Also known as the Volstead Act; prohibited the manufacture, transportation, or sale of alcohol.

19th Amendment	Granted women the right to vote.
36°30'	The line that divided the Louisiana Territory. All territory above 36°30' latitude (except Missouri) would become free states and all territory below 36°30' would become slave states.
38th Parallel	Border between North Korea (which was communist) and South Korea (which was not).
54°40' or Fight	Campaign slogan by James Polk which promised that the United States would take all of the Oregon Territory; the territory was eventually divided with the British at 49°40'.
ABC-1 Agreement	Agreement between the U.S. and Britain during WWII. The plan was to focus on defeating the Germans first, then defeating the Japanese.
Abolition	The reform movement to end slavery.
Abraham Lincoln Brigade	American civilians who volunteered to fight against Francisco Franco's fascist regime during the Spanish Civil War.
Acoma, Battle of	Battle that occurred in the Spanish Southwest. The conquistadores defeated the Pueblos and forced them to assimilate to Catholic teachings.
Adams, Abigail	Influential wife of John Adams; they exchanged letters while he attended the Continental Congresses. John Adams frequently sought his wife's advice. Her most famous guidance was to "remember the ladies," urging him to extend the right to vote to women. Her statement was one of first calls for women's suffrage in the nation.

Adams, John	Second president of the United States, strong federalist, passed Alien and Sedition Acts and attempted to appoint the midnight judges. He did not win reelection primarily because he refused to fight an official war against the French following the XYZ Affair.
Adams, John Quincy	President who supported the American Plan; Andrew Jackson contended that JQA's election occurred due to a corrupt bargain.
Adams-Onis Treaty	Treaty between the U.S. and Spain in which Spain ceded control of Florida to the U.S.
Addams, Jane	Founded Hull House, one of the earliest settlement houses of the Gilded Age. These houses assisted the working class (many immigrants) by teaching English, offering child care, and investigating housing, working, and sanitation issues. Most settlement house volunteers were women; they believed that to instill morality in society, women needed to be involved. This belief was used to promote the necessity of women's suffrage.
Adkins v. Children's Hospital	Supreme Court case which determined that the government could not enforce a federal minimum wage for women. While this did not overrule other progressive decisions like *Lochner v. New York,* it was a setback for women during the Progressive Era.
Admiralty Courts	Established by the British during colonial times to prosecute smugglers. Changed trial laws, removing colonists' right to a trial by jury, which had been their right as Englishmen.

Affirmative Action   A policy enacted in the early 1960s to attempt to reduce the challenges of historically disadvantaged groups. Started by prohibiting discrimination based on "race, creed, color, or national origin"; later expanded to prohibit discrimination based on sex.

Age of Reason, The   Book by Thomas Paine advancing the philosophy of deism, which holds that individuals should use reason and logic to guide their decisions rather than faith. This notion threatened to reduce church membership. In response, the Second Great Awakening began to bring people back to church.

Agricultural Adjustment Act, Second   A New Deal law that replaced the earlier Agricultural Adjustment Act, which had been found unconstitutional. This act expanded the Soil Conservation Act and helped tenant farmers and sharecroppers through price supports.

Agricultural Adjustment Administration (AAA)   A New Deal agency created to assist farmers. One policy implemented by the agency was the Agricultural Adjustment Act, which attempted to increase the price of crops by reducing the supply. This was done by rewarding farmers for destroying crops through government payments. Later this practice was found to be unconstitutional.

Agricultural Marketing Act   Government assistance advocated by Herbert Hoover to help farmers. Instead, it led to overproduction and deflated the value of their produce.

Alabama, The   Confederate ship built by an English shipyard. Used as a commerce raider to attack Union merchant ships.

Alamo, Battle of the	Battle that took place in Texas between Texans and the Mexican army during the Texas Revolution. All of the Americans in the Alamo mission were killed.
Albany Congress	A meeting in which seven of the 13 colonies sent representatives to meet with the Iroquois to discuss the plans for war against the French and the concept of home rule. However, the British and the colonists both had problems with the plan, and as a result, it was not implemented.
Albany Plan	Created by Benjamin Franklin, the goal was to create a unified government for the colonies which would allow for home rule.
Alger, Horatio	Author; wrote a series of fictional books. The main theme was the characters were able to go from rags to riches, a theme that supported social Darwinism.
Alien and Sedition Acts	Laws passed by President Adams to weaken the Anti-Federalists. The Alien Act forced immigrants (a group that typically supported Anti-Federalists) to wait 14 years until they could vote; it had been five years. The Sedition Act made it illegal for an American to speak against the government (which was controlled by the Federalist party).
Allied Forces (Allies)	The most powerful nations fighting against fascist nations during World War II. Included Great Britain, France, Russia, and the United States.
Alphabet Agencies	Government agencies created by the New Deal. The multitude of acronyms led to the alphabet nickname.

American Anti-Slavery Society	Abolitionist society whose creation was inspired by William Lloyd Garrison.
American Colonization Society	Organization that assisted freed slaves to return to Africa, specifically Liberia.
American Federation of Labor (AFL)	A union for skilled workers. Instead of organizing one industry, this union combined different industries that would support each other. The major requirement was that the workers be involved in skilled labor. It was led by Samuel Gompers and focused on bread and butter issues.
American Letters	Letters sent by immigrants to their friends and relatives in their native lands. Increased immigration due to the positive descriptions of America.
American Plan	Policy used by employers in the 1920s which was hostile to unions. Included the implementation of open shops and yellow dog contracts.
American Protective Association (APA)	An anti-Catholic, anti-immigrant society formed during the Gilded Age. Its purpose was to elect Protestant candidates to political office to ensure that Catholic politicians could not infuse their religious beliefs into the American government.
American Revolution	War between the American colonists and the British over economic, political, and ideological disagreements. The colonists sought independence from the British. After the colonists' victory, they gained their independence when the British signed the Treaty of Paris.

American Slavery As It Is	Book by Theodore Dwight Weld supporting the abolition of slavery. Weld wrote about real-life events illustrating the brutal conditions of slavery. The book was widely read; the only anti-slavery book read more widely was *Uncle Tom's Cabin*.
American System	A three-part plan which included a strong national banking system, protective tariffs, and improvements in infrastructure. Advocated by Henry Clay, also supported by John Quincy Adams.
American Temperance Society	Organization that began the temperance movement dedicated to eliminating the consumption of alcohol.
Anglo-Powhatan Wars	A series of wars between English settlers in the Virginia colony and the Powhatan Indians. After the wars, the Powhatans were forced to leave the eastern lands of Virginia. The two sides lived peacefully until Bacon's Rebellion in 1676.
Anschluss	The annexation of Austria during Hitler's expansion of German influence in Europe before World War II. Germany benefited through access to iron ore mines, which provided raw materials to produce steel for the German military. Germany used Austria's wealth (twice as large as Germany's wealth) to build its military. Since no nations attempted to stop Hitler's conquest, he was emboldened to take over other European countries.
Anthony, Susan B.	Women's rights advocate. Famous for her efforts in the women's suffrage movement.

Anthracite Coal Miners' Strike	The coal miners' union demanded higher wages, shorter hours, and recognition of their union. Mine owners refused these demands, and a strike occurred in 1902. Without coal, city dwellers could not heat their homes. President Roosevelt considered resolving the strike by nationalizing the mines and operating them with the Army. The strike was resolved when a government commission reduced the workday to nine hours (the union wanted eight) and provided a 10% pay raise (the union wanted 20%). This decision was viewed as a progressive victory for organized labor.
Antietam, Battle of	The Union claimed victory after this Civil War battle. This allowed Abraham Lincoln to deliver the Emancipation Proclamation. The Confederate loss also kept the British from supporting them.
Anti-Federalists	A group that opposed the Constitution over fears that the national government would be too strong. Anti-Federalists preferred a strong state government. They agreed to the Constitution only after a promise that the Bill of Rights would be added. The Anti-Federalists later became known as the Democratic-Republican party. Thomas Jefferson was one of the most prominent leaders of this political party.
Antinomianism	Anne Hutchinson's belief that those who were predestined did not need to follow the laws of God nor man. Led to her exile.

Apaches	Indian tribe, led by Geronimo, that fought fiercely to avoid removal from its land. Eventually relocated to Florida.
Apollo	U.S. space mission during the Cold War. Led to the first humans to land on the moon.
Appeal to the Colored Citizens of the World	The first document opposing slavery written by a black man. The pamphlet, written by David Walker, challenged racism, advocated for equal rights, and identified the consequences of slavery. Walker called for people of color to defy the oppression of slavery rather than to accept it.
Appeasement	Policy followed by Neville Chamberlain in which he conceded land to German aggression throughout Europe in an attempt to avoid a devastating war.
Appomattox Court House	Location where Confederate General Lee surrendered to Union General Grant. This signified the end of the Civil War.
Armada	Fleet of ships; for historical purposes, the Spanish fleet that was defeated by the British allowing Britain to create colonies in North America.
Armed Neutrality	Policy created by Catherine the Great of Russia to ally European nations to influence the British to allow freedom of the seas during the American Revolution. Important to the colonists so they could continue to trade and use their profits to support the war effort.

Army-McCarthy Hearings	Hearings which investigated Senator Joseph McCarthy's claim that members of the military were communist. The hearings showed McCarthy's accusations were baseless, and he was censured by the Senate.
Arnold, Benedict	American general during the Revolutionary War. Led the colonists in the significant battle of Valcour Island. Known as a traitor after defecting to the British Army.
Arsenal	Storehouse for weapons.
Arthur, Chester A.	Became president after the assassination of James Garfield. Established the Pendleton Act to try to reduce corruption and patronage.
Arthur, T.S.	Temperance advocate and author of *Ten Nights in a Bar-Room*, a fictional account of the effects of drinking. Each character at the bar falls victim to a calamity, and the desire for the Maine Law is repeatedly called for.
Articles of Confederation	Defined the first government of the United States. Found success in land laws; otherwise ineffective primarily due to the weakness of the federal government.
Association, The	An agreement by the American colonies to boycott British goods.
Assumption	The transfer of debt from the states to the federal government; implemented by Alexander Hamilton.

Atomic Bomb	Nuclear weapon developed by J. Robert Oppenheimer through the Manhattan Project. The first atomic bomb, named Little Boy, was dropped on Hiroshima; the second, named Fat Man, was dropped on Nagasaki. These bombings led to the death of approximately 200,000 Japanese civilians and troops. This brought about the end of World War II in the Pacific.
Awful Disclosures of Maria Monk	Book by Maria Monk intended to foster distrust and hatred against Catholics. Monk claimed that priests were forcing nuns to have sex with them; if a baby was born, it would be killed. The book is viewed as a sensationalist work fabricated to stoke prejudice against Catholics.
Axis Powers	WWII alliance among Germany, Italy, and Japan.
Aztecs	Powerful Indian empire in Mexico. They were defeated by conquistadores led by Hernán Cortés.
Bacon's Rebellion	Unsuccessful attempt by indentured servants to overthrow William Berkeley and the colonial government of Virginia. This uprising led to the use of slaves rather than indentured servants in the hopes of avoiding future rebellions.
***Ballot or the Bullet* Speech**	Speech made by Malcolm X in which he explained that if African Americans were not given the right to vote, the result would be violence.

Bank Holiday	Period of four days when Franklin Roosevelt closed all U.S. banks. Along with other banking measures passed during the holiday, it stopped withdrawals and increased consumer confidence in banks, which prevented them from being closed permanently.
Bank of the United States	National banking system created by Alexander Hamilton. Meant to strengthen the federal government. Was considered unconstitutional by Thomas Jefferson, who supported a strict constructionist interpretation of the Constitution.
Bank War	Period when Andrew Jackson eliminated the Bank of the United States before its charter had been completed.
Barbary Pirates	Pirates located on the North Coast of Africa who attacked ships traveling through the Mediterranean Sea for trade purposes. Eventually defeated by the U.S. during the Tripolitan War.
Bay of Pigs Invasion	Secret invasion of Cuba to overthrow Fidel Castro which took place during the Kennedy Administration. It was a failure.
Belligerent Nations	Term for nations at war.
Berkeley, William	Governor of Virginia. Would not protect former indentured servants who had moved west from Indian attacks. Instead Berkeley focused all his attention on the elites who lived in eastern Virginia.
Berlin Airlift	Response to the Berlin Blockade. The U.S. and allies dropped supplies to the people of West Berlin for over a year to contain the spread of communism.

Berlin Blockade	Attempt by the Soviet Union to cut off supplies to West Berlin in an effort to gain control of the entire city of Berlin.
Berlin Wall	Wall built by the East German government to prevent people in communist East Berlin from defecting to democratic West Berlin.
Bicameral Legislature	Two houses; specifically, the two houses of Congress: the House of Representatives and the Senate.
Biddle, Nicholas	President of the Bank of the United States. Challenged President Jackson during the Bank War.
Bien Dien Phu, Battle of	This battle occurred during the First Indochina War. In this battle, the Vietnamese defeated the French, which led to the French withdrawal from Vietnam. It also divided Vietnam at the 17th parallel with the agreement that elections would one day reunify the country.
Big Three	Term given for Winston Churchill, Franklin Roosevelt, and Joseph Stalin during WWII.
Bill of Rights	First ten amendments to the Constitution. Outlines the rights of individuals. Put in place due to Anti-Federalist concerns.
Birmingham, Alabama	Regarded as the most racist city in America during the Civil Rights era. Location of a protest led by Martin Luther King, Jr.

Birth of a Nation	Racist film produced by D.W. Griffith. In this film, members of the KKK are portrayed as heroic defenders of white women who were in danger from the sexual desires of black men. This film was watched widely throughout the United States and helped revive the KKK during the 1920s.
Black Codes	Economic regulations created during Reconstruction meant to preserve the traditional Southern economy. Did not allow freedmen to own or rent land or to serve on juries.
Black Panther Party for Self-Defense	Organization created by Huey Newton and Bobby Seale for the protection of black Americans from the police. It advocated that African Americans should carry guns for self-defense and to monitor the Oakland police force. Created social programs like breakfast programs for children.
Black Power	Movement led by Stokely Carmichael. Emphasized black pride and often espoused the notion that black separatism was needed.
Black Tuesday	The day the stock market crashed in 1929, leading to the Great Depression.
Blacklist	A list that union advocates were placed on during the Red Scare to prevent them from securing employment.
Blank Check	Power given to the president by Congress to spend as much money as he wants. Refers to Franklin D. Roosevelt.

Bleeding Kansas	Statewide fighting that occurred between abolitionists and slave owners in Kansas before the outbreak of the Civil War.
Bolshevik Revolution	Movement led by Vladimir Lenin which overthrew the Russian czars and created communist Russia. Led to an early exit from WWI by Russia, which made U.S. involvement even more vital.
Border Ruffians	Slave holders who crossed from Missouri to Kansas to illegally cast votes for Kansas to become a slave state. Led to Bleeding Kansas.
Border States	Slave states located between the Union and Confederacy which remained loyal to the Union during the Civil War. This was important for the Union because they had large populations, navigable rivers, and supplies that were extremely useful during the war.
Boss Tweed	Boss of the Tammany Hall political machine. Due to his corrupt practices, he was vilified in Thomas Nast's political cartoons and was eventually sent to prison by evidence produced by Samuel Tilden.
Boston Massacre	British troops murdered five colonists who were protesting the Townshend Acts. This made colonists believe the British were in the colonies to control them. It also created concern that the British would take away their natural rights, in this case the right to life.
Boston Port Act	Part of the Intolerable Acts. The British government closed the Port of Boston as punishment for the Boston Tea Party.

Boston Tea Party	The Sons of Liberty threw barrels of tea into Boston Harbor to protest the tax the British had placed upon tea.
Bourne, Randolph	A cultural pluralist whose ideas gained traction during the 1920s. Believed that the various cultures created a better, more complex culture.
Bracero Program	A program which allowed Mexican workers to enter the U.S. and fill the jobs of American men fighting in WWII. This program was essential to ensure enough food was produced for soldiers and citizens during WWII.
Brain Trust	A group of experts appointed to help Franklin Roosevelt address the Great Depression.
Bread and Butter Issues	Essential issues for all workers. Typically referred to wages and working conditions.
Brezhnev, Leonid	Leader of the Soviet Union from 1964-1982. Worked with Nixon to ease tensions between the U.S. and the Soviet Union through détente.
Brinkmanship	Strategy employed by John F. Kennedy during the Cuban Missile Crisis. Kennedy refused to negotiate or rescind his ultimatum to Nikita Khrushchev regarding Soviet missiles delivered to Cuba, forcing Khrushchev to remove the missiles or go to war.
Brooks, Preston	Member of the House of Representatives; used his cane to beat Senator Charles Sumner for insulting comments Sumner made in a speech.

Brown v. Board of Education	Supreme Court case heard by the Warren Court which determined that "separate was inherently unequal." This ruling declared that segregated schools were unconstitutional and, as a result, overruled *Plessy v. Ferguson*.
Brown, John	Abolitionist who led antislavery combatants during Bleeding Kansas and attempted to lead an armed insurrection by attacking the arsenal at Harpers Ferry. He was captured and hung for treason. Brown became a martyr for abolitionists.
Bryan, William Jennings	Populist and presidential candidate. Believed in the unlimited coinage of silver. Famously delivered the *Cross of Gold* speech.
Buchanan, James	President of the United States. Did not try to stop southern states from seceding after the election of Abraham Lincoln (Buchanan was a lame duck president when South Carolina seceded; Lincoln had not yet been inaugurated).
Buena Vista, Battle of	Key American victory during the Mexican War; ensured the eventual American victory in the war.
Buford, The	Also called the *Soviet Ark*. Ship that deported 249 non-citizens who were alleged communist sympathizers during the Red Scare of the 1920s.
Bulge, Battle of the	Surprise attack by German forces to attempt to gain control of the port of Antwerp. The Germans were unsuccessful and sustained massive casualties. As a result, this was the last German offensive campaign during World War II.

Bull Moose Party	During the presidential election of 1912, former president Theodore Roosevelt challenged current president William Howard Taft for the Republican nomination. When Taft defeated him, Roosevelt created his own political party, the Bull Moose party. This divided Republican voters, which allowed Democratic candidate Woodrow Wilson to win the presidency.
Bull Run, Battle of	First major land battle of the Civil War. The Confederacy won which made the Union take the war more seriously.
Bull Run, Second Battle of	A major victory for the Confederacy that emboldened Robert E. Lee to attack north into Maryland where he suffered a defeat at Antietam.
Bunker Hill, Battle of	Battle that occurred before the Revolutionary War officially began. Although the British took the hill, they suffered huge casualties and showed their poor leadership and overconfidence.
Burgoyne, John	General in the British military during the Revolutionary War. After winning the Battle of Valcour Island, Burgoyne made the mistake of returning to Canada for the winter instead of remaining in New York. As a result of their absence, the British lost control of the territory and had to attempt to regain control of it in the spring.
Burned-Over District	Area of New England where the majority of camp meetings took place during the Second Great Awakening.

Butternut Region	Areas of southern Illinois, Ohio, and Indiana that opposed the anti-slavery aspect of the Civil War.
Calhoun, John C.	U.S. Senator and Vice President. Wrote the South Carolina Exposition and was important in the passage of the Compromise of 1850.
California Bear Flag Republic	Name for California for a short time during the Mexican War.
California Gold Rush	In 1848 gold was found at Sutter's Mill. This began the gold rush of 1849, which led to a massive population increase as well as a substantial amount of crime.
Calvin, John	Important figure in the Protestant Reformation. Believed in the concept of predestination.
Cambodia	Nation in southeast Asia that borders Vietnam. In the Vietnam War, the North Vietnamese army would use eastern Cambodia as a place to rest and reorganize without fear of being attacked. Although unconstitutional without the authorization of Congress, President Nixon ordered a secret bombing campaign to attack North Vietnamese bases in Cambodia.
Camp David Accords	Peace treaty brokered by President Carter and signed by Egyptian president Anwar Sadat and Israeli Prime Minister Menachem Begin. Attempted to address territorial disputes between Israel and Palestine. Additionally, Israel gave back control of the Sinai Peninsula to Egypt.

Camp Meetings	Religious services that took place during the Second Great Awakening in fields throughout America, especially New England.
Capone, Al	Most notorious gangster during Prohibition. His gang sold alcohol and engaged in turf battles with rival gangs. This led to the St. Valentine's Day massacre; gang members, dressed like police officers, pulled over rival gang members, lined them up against an alley wall, and executed them with machine guns.
Carlisle Schools	Eastern boarding schools created to assimilate Indian children. Disease led to high levels of death.
Carmichael, Stokely	One of the original leaders of the Black Power movement.
Carnegie, Andrew	Steel magnate during the Gilded Age. Used vertical integration and Pittsburgh Plus Pricing to become extremely wealthy. Later became a philanthropist.
Carson, Rachel	Author of *Silent Spring*, which explained the hazardous effects of pesticides (e.g., DDT) on the environment. This book helped initiate the environmentalist movement in the U.S.
Carter, Jimmy	President of the United States. Successfully negotiated the Camp David Accords. Failed to end the Iranian Hostage Crisis and could not fix the American economy.
Cartwright, Peter	Circuit rider during the Second Great Awakening.

Cash and Carry	Completely ended the earlier Neutrality Acts. Sold war materials to democracies in Europe if they paid for goods in cash and transported them.
Cash Crops	Agricultural crops to be sold for a profit; contrast with subsistence crops, which are grown for consumption by the farmer and his livestock.
Castro, Fidel	Communist leader of Cuba. The U.S. attempted to overthrow him in the Bay of Pigs Invasion. He responded by requesting missiles from the U.S.S.R. which he believed could be a deterrent against future attacks. This led to the Cuban Missile Crisis.
Catherine the Great	Czar of Russia. Created armed neutrality during the American Revolution.
Central Pacific Railroad Company	Built railroads from west to east. Primarily employed Chinese laborers.
Century of Dishonor, A	Book written by Helen Hunt Jackson. Illustrated the wrongs perpetuated against Indians over 100 years of history.
Chamberlain, Neville	Prime minister of Great Britain. Followed the policy of appeasement when dealing with Hitler. Believed mistakenly that his negotiations had led to peace.
Checks and Balances	System that ensures no single branch of the U.S. government can dominate the others.
***Chesapeake* Affair**	Incident where the British demanded an American ship, the *Chesapeake*, hand over British deserters on board. When the American captain refused, the British opened fire. This incident, along with several other grievances, led to the War of 1812.

Chiang Kai-shek	Nationalist ruler of China during the civil war against the communists led by Mao Zedong.
Churchill, Winston	Prime Minister of Britain during World War II.
CIA	The Central Intelligence Agency, responsible for gathering and analyzing information for purposes of U.S. national security. During the Cold War, a key mission of the agency was to obtain information on the Soviet Union and conduct covert operations against communist nations.
Circuit Riders	Itinerant ministers who preached during the Second Great Awakening.
Civic Virtue	The quality of doing what is best for the country rather than pursuing one's own selfish desires. It was believed that women were best equipped to instill this value in their children; as a result, they were expected to stay in the home and educate their children on how to be good citizens.
Civil Rights Act of 1957	Law passed during the Eisenhower administration to placate supporters of Civil Rights while creating little meaningful change. The legislation aimed to increase voting opportunities for African Americans in southern states, but because it was difficult to enforce, voting increased by less than 3%.
Civil Rights Act of 1964	Law passed by Lyndon Johnson which banned racial discrimination in private businesses and funded desegregation in public schools.

Civil Service Exam	Merit-based test given to applicants for government jobs. Avoided patronage. Created in response to the assassination of James Garfield.
Civil War	War between the Union and the Confederacy, primarily over slavery. Began when Abraham Lincoln was elected president and South Carolina seceded.
Civil Works Administration (CWA)	A short-term job creation program created by FERA during the New Deal. Projects dealt primarily with infrastructure. Created jobs for four million people.
Civilian Conservation Corps (CCC)	Job creation program established by the New Deal. Created conservation-related jobs for three million men.
Clay, Henry	Speaker of the House, Senator, and presidential candidate. Known as the Great Compromiser for his role in the Missouri Compromise, the Compromise Tariff of 1833, and the Compromise of 1850. He supported the American System, blamed by Andrew Jackson for the alleged corrupt bargain.
Clayton Antitrust Act	Law created to combat monopolies after the earlier Sherman Antitrust Act failed. This new law was more specific in defining what actions were illegal and gave the government more enforcement power. This was a key piece of legislation during the Progressive Era.

Clean Air Act and Clean Water Act

These laws allowed the Environmental Protection Agency to protect against air and water pollution. Nixon signed the Clean Air Act and vetoed the Clean Water Act; however, Congress was able to override the veto. The laws exemplified the environmental movement started by Rachel Carson.

Cleveland, Grover

President who broke the Pullman Palace Car strike by sending in the military.

Closed Shop

A business whose workers are required to join the union. Businesses where union membership is not required are known as open shops.

Code Talkers

Navajo Indians who enlisted in the military during WWII. Their language could not be understood by the Japanese; therefore, it was an unbreakable code.

Coercive Acts

See Intolerable Acts.

Cohens v. Virginia

Supreme Court case which tried two brothers for illegally selling lottery tickets. Although the court followed the earlier decisions of the lower courts, this case was significant. It determined that the Supreme Court was the court of last resort / highest court in the nation. Exhibited federal power.

Cold War

Period of tension between the U.S. and the U.S.S.R. from 1945-1991. During this time, the two superpowers never fought against each other directly; however, they were indirectly involved in conflicts throughout the rest of the world in a battle for influence and supremacy.

Collective Bargaining	Type of negotiating in which the workers within a union choose representatives to negotiate on their behalf. The purpose is to advocate for salary, insurance, and benefits.
Columbian Exchange	Transfer of goods between Europe and the Americas. Included crops, animals, and most significantly diseases and precious metals.
Commerce Clause	States that the federal government (Congress) has authority over several aspects of commerce. Most significant for interstate commerce.
Committees of Correspondence	A secret organization throughout the colonies which helped frame the Revolutionary perspective that the British were violating their rights. Also responsible for organizing many of the actions by the colonists against the British.
Common Sense	Pamphlet written by Thomas Paine. Advocated for independence from the British. Two of Paine's major arguments were that Britain was too far away to effectively govern the colonies and that the colonies were too large for such a small island to govern.
Communism	Ideology advocating for a classless society. Became the foundation of Russian political and economic policies after the Bolshevik Revolution; created tension between the U.S. and the Soviet Union during the Cold War.

Compromise of 1850	Put in place following the Mexican War. Important aspects included a stricter fugitive slave law, popular sovereignty in new territories, and California becoming a free state.
Compromise of 1877	Settled the controversy over the election of 1876. The returns from three southern states were contested. It was assumed that, had an accurate recount been completed, the Democratic candidate, Samuel Tilden would have won. However, due to the compromise, a recount did not occur. The Republican candidate, Rutherford B. Hayes, became president; in return, Republicans agreed to remove troops from the South. This ended Reconstruction.
Compromise Tariff of 1833	Resolved the Nullification Crisis by lowering the Tariff of Abominations and the legislature of South Carolina agreeing to collect tariff duties.
Comstock Lode	A large silver deposit found in Nevada in 1859.
Concord	Colonial arsenal. The minutemen defeated the British troops, who were attempting to take the weapons stored in the arsenal.
Confederacy	Term for the southern states that seceded from the Union and created an alternative government during the Civil War.
Conquistadores	Spanish conquerors. Desired wealth and the conversion of Indians as an extension of the Reconquista in Spain.

Constitution	Defined the second government of the United States, following the Articles of Confederation. Its creation was due to Shays' Rebellion and fear of mob rule. As a result, the federal government became much more powerful. Specifically, it had the ability to tax and regulate interstate commerce, and it created an army.
Containment	Strategy created by George Kennan during the Cold War to prevent communism from spreading.
Contras	A Nicaraguan rebel group that was secretly and illegally funded by the U.S. government during the Reagan Administration. The Contras were attempting to overthrow the communist government of the Sandinistas.
Convention of 1800	Agreement between the U.S. and France to end their unofficial war. Officially ended the Franco-American alliance.
Conversion Experience	A religious experience that confirmed to the Puritans that a person was predestined.
Coolidge, Calvin	President who supported high protective tariffs and refused to help farmers struggling in the 1920s. Believed that the government should follow laissez-faire principles.
Cooper, James Fenimore	Author of *The Last of the Mohicans*. Popular after the War of 1812, it exemplified nationalist feelings that followed the war. It focused on American themes during the French and Indian War.

Coral Sea, Battle of the
Battle in the Pacific theater during World War II. It was the first battle in history in which both sides used aircraft carriers.

Cornwallis, Charles
British army officer during the American Revolution. Was defeated at the Battle of Yorktown. This signaled the coming end of the war.

Corrupt Bargain
Allegation by Andrew Jackson during the election of 1824. Jackson believed that Henry Clay made a deal with John Quincy Adams to steal the presidency from him.

Cotton Gin
Invented by Eli Whitney. Separated seeds from cotton; this helped develop the market revolution, which revived the slave system.

Counterculture
Refers to groups like the hippies who rejected traditional American values and lived alternative lifestyles.

Coureurs de Bois
French trappers and traders.

Court Packing
Effort by Franklin Roosevelt to add as many as six additional judges to the Supreme Court. He was frustrated that the Court found some of his New Deal policies unconstitutional. He proposed to add a new judge for every judge over the age of 70; however, the idea was unpopular and was not enacted.

Crimes Against Kansas, The	Speech given by Senator Charles Sumner criticizing the Kansas-Nebraska Act. Specifically attacked Senator Andrew Butler from South Carolina. This led to Representative Preston Brooks caning Senator Sumner.
Crittenden, John	Senator who proposed the Crittenden Compromise after Abraham Lincoln's election. Suggested that slave territory should be every state below 36°30' throughout the entire country. The Compromise was not enacted.
Cross of Gold Speech	Speech given by William Jennings Bryan; supported the populist policy of unlimited coinage of silver.
Cuban Missile Crisis	A 13-day confrontation during the Kennedy Administration between the U.S. and the Soviet Union over missiles the Soviets were delivering to Cuba. It had the potential to lead to war. However, the Soviet Union agreed to end delivery of missiles and remove missiles that had already been delivered. In return, the U.S. removed missiles from Turkey.
Cultural Pluralist	Opposed the restriction of immigration in the 1920s. Believed that immigration made America a better country.
Culture of Domesticity	Belief that women should stay in the home and ensure their children and husbands lived moral lives. This belief influenced women who had been working to stop working after marriage and raise their children.
Cumberland Road	First national road and main transportation west for early travelers.

Cummings, E.E.	One of the "Lost Generation" writers of the 1920s. Following World War I, the Lost Generation sought to end Victorian traditions. Cummings did this by breaking grammatical rules to show the beauty and creativity of individualism.
Custer, George	U.S. military general. Fought in Indian Wars; most famous for his defeat at the Battle of Little Bighorn, also known as Custer's Last Stand.
Dartmouth College v. Woodward	Supreme Court case. The state of New Hampshire tried unsuccessfully to convert Dartmouth College from a private to a public institution. Illustrated the significance of contracts and federal power.
Dawes Act	Also known as the Dawes Severalty Act. Allowed the U.S. government to divide Indian lands and parcel out individual allotments to Indians who met the conditions of land ownership. Led to the loss of tribal land. This policy was designed to assimilate Indians living on the reservation.
Dawes Plan	An attempt to solve the debt European nations could not repay following WWI. U.S. banks loaned money to the German government so it could make its reparation payments to European nations, most significantly France.
De Las Casas, Bartolome	Spanish priest and missionary who exposed the brutal treatment the indigenous people of the Americas were subjected to at the hands of the Spanish.
Debs, Eugene	Union leader who led the Pullman Palace Car strike in 1894.

Declaration of Independence	Document written by Thomas Jefferson stating the colonists demanded their independence from the British. The purpose of the document was to gain support from colonists, British sympathizers, and foreign nations.
Declaration of Rights and Sentiments, The	A document presented at the Seneca Falls Convention calling for equality between the genders, specifically the need to allow women the right to vote.
Declaratory Act	Law created in response to the repeal of the Stamp Act, stating that the British government could pass any law it desired. This created concern for the colonists because the British were making it clear that the natural rights and the rights of Englishmen were no longer guaranteed to the colonists.
Deep South	Geographic region including states such as Mississippi, Alabama, and Louisiana. Slavery was the most brutal in this region.
Democratic Convention of 1968	The official gathering to choose the Democratic candidate to run against Richard Nixon. Anti-war democrats protested at the convention against the nomination of Hubert Humphrey, who supported the Vietnam War. Chicago mayor Richard Daley ordered the police to contain the protests, and as protestors marched towards the convention site, the police began to attack. The chaos was captured on television and made the Democratic Party look out of control. As a result, Richard Nixon's stated position of being a law and order candidate became even more appealing to American voters.

Democratic-Republican Party	Political party initially led by Thomas Jefferson. It supported strong state governments and opposed a strong federal government.
Desegregation	Policy of integrating public and private facilities by allowing African Americans to access them. This challenged the decision of *Plessy v. Ferguson*.
Destroyer Deal	Occurred during WWII. The U.S. traded used destroyers to the British for naval bases the British controlled in the Western Hemisphere.
Détente	An easing of tensions. Occurred during the Nixon administration when foreign policy decisions helped improve relationships with communist nations. Began when Nixon had his National Security Advisor Henry Kissinger visit China. Shortly afterwards, he was invited to visit the Soviet Union.
Direct Tax	A tax assessed on a good produced within the colonies. Resisted by colonists because they were not represented in Parliament, the British political body that created the direct tax.
Dissenter	A person who challenged government and religious authority in colonial New England.
Dix, Dorothea	Reformer who improved the treatment of the mentally ill.
Dole, The	Welfare; associated with the Great Depression.

Domino Theory	Theory that if one nation in Southeast Asia turned communist, neighboring countries would also turn communist, like a chain of dominoes falling over. Primary reason the U.S. got involved in the Vietnam War.
Double V Campaign	African-American campaign during WWII to win the war and eliminate racist policies in the U.S.
Douglas, Stephen	Created the Kansas-Nebraska Act. Participated in the Lincoln-Douglas debates and won the race for U.S. Senate.
Douglass, Frederick	An escaped slave and prominent abolitionist. Wrote his autobiography *The Narrative Life of Frederick Douglass*. This book was influential because it gave Northerners who had never visited the South a stronger idea of the horrors of slavery.
Dred Scott v. Sandford	Supreme Court case that stated Dred Scott, a slave, was not free even if his master took him to a free soil state. This decision made the claim that free soil did not truly exist. This led to an uproar because it negated earlier compromises such as the Missouri Compromise and the Compromise of 1850. It also nullified the Northwest Ordinance.
Du Bois, W.E.B.	Civil rights leader during the late 1800s and early 1900s. He disagreed with the accommodationist policies of Booker T. Washington and insisted on full equality for African Americans by giving the Talented 10% immediate equality to prove their abilities.

Dust Bowl	Period of profound drought during the 1920s and 1930s which led to dust storms which destroyed farms; usually associated with Kansas and Oklahoma.
Earth Day	Founded by Wisconsin senator Gaylord Nelson to educate Americans about the environment. On the first Earth Day in 1970, 20 million Americans demonstrated in their communities for healthy environment. This led to several environmental laws being passed in the 1970s.
Edwards, Jonathan	Minister during the Great Awakening. Famous for his sermon *Sinners in the Hands of an Angry God*. Preached about hellfire and brimstone with the intent of instilling the fear of God in his listeners.
Eisenhower, Dwight	President of the United States for the majority of the 1950s. Ended the Korean War and tried to avoid the Civil Rights struggle but was forced to assert federal power by sending troops to Little Rock, Arkansas.
El Alamein, Battle of	Battle in Egypt fought by the British in which they defeated the Axis and protected access to the Suez Canal. This prevented the Axis powers from gaining control of Middle East oil fields.
Elastic Clause	Also known as the Necessary and Proper clause. Statement in the Constitution that allows Congress to extend its powers beyond what is stated in the Constitution to carry out what is necessary and proper. Allowed for the creation of a Bank of the United States.

Electoral College	System of indirectly choosing a president in the United States. Initially created to allow electors to ignore voters in their state if they felt the voters had made a poor choice. This system has led to a candidate who did not win the popular vote to become president five times in American history.
Elkins Act	Example of a Progressive Era reform that levied heavy fines on railroads that offered rebates and on businessmen who accepted the rebates.
Emancipation Proclamation	Speech delivered by Abraham Lincoln after the Union victory at Antietam, stating that slaves in the Confederacy were free. Despite this declaration, slavery continued in the Confederate states, and it was still allowed in the border states. Therefore, it would be more accurate to observe that the 13th Amendment is what truly freed the slaves.
Embargo Act	Enacted by Thomas Jefferson. Ended trade with all nations in an attempt to stop naval attacks by the British and French as well as British impressment. Hurt the American economy more than it affected the British or the French economies.
Emergency Banking Relief Act	Depression-era law that allowed banks to open if they could prove to the government they were financially stable.
Emergency Quota Act of 1921	Restricted immigration in the U.S. during the 1920s Red Scare. The number of new immigrants from any country was limited each year to 3% of the number of people from that same country who resided in the United States as of the 1910 census.

Enclosure	The policy of fencing previously accessible land in England. Forced many small farmers and shepherds to become indentured servants.
Encomienda System	Created by the Spanish to enslave Indians on a plantation and allowed the Spanish to profit from the cultivation of cash crops. Also required the Spanish to convert the Indians on their land to Catholicism.
Enlightenment	Philosophical movement in Europe. Several ideas were embraced by American colonists and eventually led to a desire to declare independence. The most notable was the idea of natural rights created by John Locke.
Entangling Alliances	Mentioned in George Washington's Farewell Address. Warning to Americans to avoid alliances with European nations. This continued to show Washington's commitment to isolation.
Environmental Protection Agency (EPA)	Federal agency that regulates laws intended to protect Americans' health and the environment.
Equal Rights Amendment	Proposed amendment to the U.S. Constitution. Purpose was to guarantee equal treatment to all regardless of gender. It never passed.
Era of Good Feelings	Period following the War of 1812, so named because the bitter partisanship between the Federalists and Democratic-Republicans appeared to be reduced. Additionally, there was a strong sense of nationalism and unity.

Erie Canal	Manmade waterway connecting the Great Lakes to the interior of New York State. Construction occurred under Governor Dewitt Clinton.
Escalation	Occurred during Lyndon Johnson's presidency. His plan to win the Vietnam War was to increase the number of U.S. troops dramatically (from 75,000 to 125,000).
Evers, Medgar	Civil rights activist in Mississippi who worked for the NAACP, murdered by a member of the KKK.
Evolution	Scientific concept advanced by Charles Darwin positing that species evolve. This created controversy, as it instigated a debate between religion and science.
Excise Tax	One aspect of Alexander Hamilton's fiscal policy to generate revenue. A direct tax on whiskey, which led to the Whiskey Rebellion. Immediately repealed by Jefferson when he became president.
Executive Order 9066	Implemented by Franklin Roosevelt after the bombing of Pearl Harbor. This act, created out of fear and prejudice, forced Japanese-Americans living on the west coast to leave their homes and be imprisoned in internment camps.
Fair Deal	Harry Truman's plan to assist the American people, similar to the New Deal. Among several other goals, he hoped to increase employment, improve access to housing, and support veterans returning from war. Few of his goals were realized due to opposition by Republicans and Dixiecrats.

Fair Labor Standards Act	Law enacted during Franklin Roosevelt's presidency that created a minimum wage and overtime pay at a rate of "time and a half" when employees involved in interstate commerce work over 40 hours a week. Also outlawed most types of child labor.
Falwell, Jerry	Founder of the conservative organization the Moral Majority. The organization organized Christians to vote as a political bloc, typically in support of Republican candidates. This organization was operational throughout the 1980s and is an example of the New Right.
Farewell Address	Written by George Washington at the end of his presidency. Urged Americans to avoid the creation of political parties and to avoid entangling alliances.
Farmers' Alliance	First national organization of farmers. Sponsored social events and organized cooperatives. Led to the rise of the Populists.
Faubus, Orval	Governor of Arkansas. Called in the National Guard to prevent the Little Rock Nine from attending Central High School, a battle of federal versus state power. As a result, Eisenhower sent in troops to escort the nine black students into the school.
FDIC	Federal Deposit Insurance Corporation. Agency that provides insurance on deposits (money) placed in banks. Established during the Great Depression by Franklin Roosevelt.
Federal Emergency Relief Act	Created FERA, a federal agency that distributed money to states during the Great Depression. The money was meant for job creation and the dole.

Federal Highway Act	Enacted by Dwight Eisenhower. Created the interstate highway system.
Federal Housing Administration	Governmental agency created during the New Deal. Implemented policies that stabilized the banking industry through regulating and encouraging home loans.
Federal Reserve	National banking system of the U.S. created during the Wilson presidency. Its purpose is to avoid panics and to enact policies to stabilize the economy when problems in the economy arise.
Federalist Papers	Collection of essays written to persuade the New York legislature to accept the Constitution as a new form of government.
Federalists	Americans who supported a strong national government. Prominent federalists included Alexander Hamilton, John Adams, and John Marshall.
Finney, Charles Grandison	Minister during the Second Great Awakening.
Fireside Chats	Radio shows held by Franklin Roosevelt meant to restore confidence to the American people.
First Continental Congress	Meeting of delegates from the colonies. During this meeting, the colonists listed their rights and began the Association.

First Indochina War	War that took place following World War II between the French and the Vietnamese who sought independence. The U.S. supported the French and took over the war effort after France was defeated at the Battle of Dien Bien Phu.
Fitzgerald, F. Scott	Most famous of the Lost Generation authors of the 1920s. Wrote *This Side of Paradise* and *The Great Gatsby*. His stories, like the other authors of the Lost Generation, showed disillusionment.
Flapper	A young woman in the 1920s who exhibited her social independence by wearing a bob haircut, short skirts, and lipstick; who smoked, drank, and went to dancehalls.
Flexible Response	John F. Kennedy's policy to have varying methods to respond to military threats.
Focus on the Family	Conservative religious organization, part of the New Right movement of the 1980s. Opposed gay rights, supported abstinence-only education and traditional gender roles, and advocated against divorce.
Force Acts	Sent troops to southern states to act as a police force and protect southern blacks during Reconstruction.
Force Bill	Imposed by Andrew Jackson after the Compromise Tariff of 1833. Declared the military could be used to enforce the collection of tariffs. Showed the supremacy of the federal government over the state government.

Ford, Gerald	Became president when Richard Nixon resigned; ended U.S. involvement in the Vietnam War; pardoned Nixon.
Fordney-McCumber Tariff	A tax that raised tariffs on many imported goods to 38.5%. Greatly restricted international trade.
Fort Donelson, Battle of	Location of a battle in the Western Theater during the Civil War. The battle was won by Ulysses S. Grant and ensured that the Union would have access to the Cumberland River, which was vital for transportation.
Fort Henry, Battle of	First significant victory for the Union during the Civil War. The battle was won by Ulysses S. Grant.
Fort Sumter	A Union fort in South Carolina. It was surrounded by the Confederate Army. Lincoln attempted to resupply the fort, and as a result, the Confederacy attacked and gained the fort but strengthened support for the Union by Northerners.
Franco, Francisco	A fascist Spanish general who led a successful military rebellion and ruled over Spain.
Franco-American Alliance	An alliance between the colonists and the French to be united in defeating the British. George Washington did not honor this alliance during the French Revolution and the alliance was eliminated in the Convention of 1800.
Franklin, Benjamin	Colonial leader who tried to create home rule through the Albany Plan.

Frazier-Lemke Farm Bankruptcy Act	A law passed during the Great Depression to protect farmers from losing their homes and farms. Stopped banks from repossessing farms for five years if the owner couldn't make a mortgage payment. Was found unconstitutional by the Supreme Court.
Free Soil Party	Political party that opposed the expansion of slavery into the western territories. Later evolved into the Republican Party.
Freedman's Bureau	Established by Congress after the Civil War to provide food, clothing, medical care, and education to the freedmen. However, was successful only in providing education.
Freedmen	Freed slaves after the Civil War.
Freedom Riders	Civil rights advocates who rode Greyhound buses from the North to the South to challenge laws on segregation. They were attacked which forced the federal government to protect them since this was interstate commerce.
Freedom Summer	Volunteer campaign created in 1964 to help register black voters in the south.
Freeport Doctrine	Stephen Douglas's statement during the Lincoln-Douglas debates that challenged the Dred Scott decision. Douglas stated that slaves could not be brought to free soil states.
Freeport Question	Question posed by Abraham Lincoln to Stephen Douglas asking if slavery could exist on free soil.

French and Indian War	War fought by the colonists and the British against the French and their Indian allies for control over the Ohio River Valley.
Friedan, Betty	Leader in the women's rights movement. Wrote *The Feminine Mystique* in 1963, which focused on many women's issues including the idea that women had a desire for a life outside of the home.
Frontier Thesis	Written by Frederick Jackson Turner. Claimed the frontier was closed and this created a threat to democracy.
Fugitive Slave Law	Part of the Compromise of 1850. Stated that Northerners would have to help capture runaway slaves. Also instituted a rule that the magistrates hearing cases of alleged runaway slaves would be paid $5 for a "not guilty" verdict and $10 for a "guilty" verdict.
Fulton, Robert	Inventor of the steamboat, which allowed ships to travel with and against the current, thus improving transportation. The steamboat was an important part of the transportation revolution, which aided the Market Revolution.
Funding at Par	Policy instituted by Alexander Hamilton. Promised the U.S. would repay its debts.
Gadsden Purchase	The purchase of a section of land that was part of northern Mexico and became part of Arizona. The purpose was to build a transcontinental railroad which would pass through this area. This land and the possibility of the railroad led to the Kansas-Nebraska Act.

Garfield, James	President who was assassinated by a man who believed that Garfield should have given him a government job (patronage).
Garrison, William Lloyd	Abolitionist and editor of *The Liberator*. Called for the immediate and uncompensated end to slavery.
Geronimo	Apache leader who fought against the U.S. military during the Indian wars during the Gilded Age.
Gettysburg, Battle of	Civil War battle that took place in Pennsylvania. The Confederates lost what was the bloodiest battle in the war. This battle, combined with the loss at Vicksburg, convinced the British government to prevent the delivery of the Laird Rams to the Confederacy.
Ghent, Treaty of	Ended the War of 1812. Ushered in over 200 years of relative peace between the U.S. and Britain.
Ghost Dance	A Lakota religious ritual meant to allow communication with dead spirits. When the U.S. army learned of the Ghost Dance taking place at Wounded Knee, they massacred the Indians in attendance, which included women and children.
GI Bill	Provided funding to soldiers returning from WWII to attend college or technical school. The funds were given primarily to white veterans due to racist policies. By 1946 only one-fifth of the 100,000 black servicemen had been admitted to college.

Gibbons v. Ogden	Supreme Court case. Determined the state of New York could not give a monopoly to a steamboat company. Showed supremacy of federal government over state government.
Gideon v. Wainwright	Supreme Court case heard by the Warren Court. Determined that those arrested had a right to a lawyer.
Gilded Age	Historical period that lasted from approximately 1865 to 1900. The era is associated with corruption and greed.
Glasnost	A policy of openness implemented by Mikhail Gorbachev. Showed that communism was becoming less strict in Russia.
Glass-Steagall Banking Reform Act	Enacted during the Great Depression; separated commercial and investment banking. It also established the FDIC, which insured bank deposits. This helped renew trust in the banking system.
Gold Standard	A monetary system based on gold. This system was challenged by indebted farmers during the Gilded Age. They advocated for a gold and silver standard which would allow for inflation to occur which would allow them to pay their debts off easier. This was opposed by bankers and industrialists.
Goliad, Battle of	Battle that occurred during the Texas Revolution. When the Texans were defeated, they threw down their weapons, and the Mexican army executed them. This led to anger throughout the U.S. and more Americans came to fight in Texas.

Gompers, Samuel	President of the American Federation of Labor.
Good Neighbor Policy	Foreign policy of Franklin Roosevelt towards Latin America. Marked a transition away from the dominance the U.S. had exerted over Latin America in the past.
Gorbachev, Mikhail	Leader of the Soviet Union. Enacted reforms which led to the end of communism in Russia.
Gospel of Wealth	The perspective promoted by Andrew Carnegie which states that the wealthy have a responsibility to redistribute their money through philanthropy.
Gould, Jay	Leading railroad developer and speculator during the Gilded Age. Used unethical methods such as stock watering to increase his fortune.
Grandfather Clause	Allowed southern men to vote without paying a poll tax or a literacy test if their grandfathers had been able to vote. The purpose was to allow all white men to vote while stopping black men from voting.
Grangers	Farmers who organized in an effort to increase their political and economic power.
Grant, Ulysses S.	Successful Union general during the Civil War. Unsuccessful president after the war; although he was not corrupt, many in his administration were.
Great Awakening	A religious revival which occurred in the 1730s and 1740s. It gave the colonists a unifying experience.

Great Compromise	A blending of the New Jersey and Virginia Plans. It created a bicameral legislature: the lower chamber based on population, the upper chamber had equal representation from each state.
Great Depression	A period of severe economic hardship that occurred primarily during the 1930s caused by buying stocks on margin (a form of overspeculation).
Great Migration	The movement of southern blacks to the North during WWI and WWII in search of improved economic opportunities and less racist treatment.
Great Railroad Strike of 1877	Occurred after the railroad cut wages for the third time in a year. It ended when President Hayes sent U.S. troops to end the strike.
Great Society	Domestic plan of Lyndon Johnson. The purpose was to end poverty and combat racism.
Greene, Nathanael	Officer in the Continental army during the American Revolution. Successfully led his men in the southern theater of war by employing guerrilla tactics. He engaged with the enemy when he had the advantage and retreated when in danger. This allowed him to significantly weaken the British forces with minimal casualties to his own men.
Grimke, Sarah Moore	Member of the women's suffrage movement. A prolific writer; spoke frequently at public meetings.
Guadalupe Hidalgo, Treaty of	Treaty that ended the Mexican War and resulted in the U.S. acquiring the Mexican Cession.

Guiteau, Charles	Assassinated President Garfield. He believed that by assassinating Garfield (who was part of the Half-Breed faction of the Republican party), he would be rewarded with a government appointment by Chester A. Arthur (who was part of the Stalwart faction and was now president). Instead, he was executed. The Pendleton Act was then enacted to ensure government jobs were awarded on merit.
Gulf of Tonkin	Body of water that borders Vietnam. President Johnson claimed that the North Vietnamese fired on American ships. This led to the America's open involvement in the Vietnam War. It was later found that Johnson's claims were exaggerated.
Haight-Ashbury	A neighborhood in San Francisco made famous during the Summer of Love. This neighborhood is credited with being the site where the hippie counterculture movement originated.
Half-Breeds	A faction of the Republican Party during the Gilded Age.
Hamilton, Alexander	Secretary of the Treasury. Instituted several economic policies meant to strengthen the federal government.
Harding, Warren G.	President during the early 1920s. His administration was known for corruption, specifically the Teapot Dome Scandal.
Harlem Renaissance	Period marked by the production of great works of culture (literature, art, music) during the 1920s in the Harlem neighborhood of New York. Strengthened black pride.

Harpers Ferry	Location of an arsenal that John Brown attacked in the hopes of starting a slave rebellion. John Brown was captured here.
Hartford Convention	Meetings where Federalists in New England declared an ultimatum in response to opposition to the War of 1812. They threatened that if their demands were not met, they would secede from the nation. However, rather than forcing the government to give into their desires, they lost status, and this event became known as the death of the Federalist Party.
Hawley-Smoot Tariff	Under President Herbert Hoover, increased the tax on imports from 38.5% to 60%. Led to a trade war that devastated the world economy.
Hayes, Rutherford B.	President of the United States who received fewer popular votes and potentially fewer electoral votes. However, he became president due to the Compromise of 1877.
Haymarket Square Riot	Site of 1886 labor protest held by the Knights of Labor. An anarchist detonated a bomb, killing eight. Although the bombing had nothing to do with the Knights of Labor, they were blamed for it, and this ended the Knights of Labor.
Headright System	Land given to anyone who paid the cost of transportation of an indentured servant to America. Led to land in eastern Virginia being taken, which forced the freed indentured servants to move west.

Helper, Hinton	Author of *The Impending Crisis of the South.* Accurately explained that slavery harmed most southern whites economically.
Hepburn Act	Strengthened the Interstate Commerce Commission's ability to regulate the railroads. Allowed the Commission to set a maximum rate for shipping and outlawed free passes.
Hessians	German mercenaries who fought for the British during the American Revolution.
Hippies	Members of a counterculture group during the 1960s, known for communal living, drug use, free love, and protesting the war in Vietnam.
Hiroshima	Japanese city where the first atomic bomb was dropped.
Hiss, Alger	American government official wrongly accused of being a communist spy during the 1950s Red Scare.
Hitler, Adolf	Leader of Germany during WWII. Murdered up to six million Jews during the Holocaust.
Hitler-Stalin Pact	Agreement between Germany and Russia not to attack each other leading into WWII.
Ho Chi Minh	Nationalist leader of North Vietnam during the Vietnam War.
Hoover, Herbert	President during the early stages of the Great Depression. Feared too much assistance would weaken Americans' resolve.

Hooverville	Shantytowns built during the Great Depression due to homelessness. The term Hooverville was meant to mock President Hoover who was unable to improve the condition of poor Americans.
Horizontal Integration	Type of monopoly used by John D. Rockefeller with his Standard Oil empire. Rockefeller bought smaller oil companies until he controlled 95% of all oil in the U.S.
Housing and Urban Development, Department of	Also known as HUD. U.S. government agency tasked with improving housing and urban renewal.
How the Other Half Lives	Photo book by Jacob Riis during the Progressive Era. Exposed the terrible conditions of slums and inspired housing reforms during the Reform Era.
HUAC	House Un-American Activities Committee, which gained notoriety during the 1950s Red Scare. Its stated purpose was to investigate possible communists; became a witch hunt.
Hudson River School	First American art movement. Artists focused on painting American landscapes. Illustrated the nationalist pride that existed after the War of 1812.
Hughes, Langston	African-American writer during the Harlem Renaissance. Wrote in a style that supported pride and hope in the black community.
Hull House	A settlement house operated by Jane Addams opened in during the Gilded Age. The purpose was to assist immigrants.

Humanitarian Diplomacy	Jimmy Carter's foreign policy plan, which promoted human rights and respect for other nations' governments.
Humphrey, Hubert	Democratic candidate who won the primary in 1968. He supported the war in Vietnam; as a result, a protest occurred at the Democratic Convention in Chicago. This disorder helped the Republican candidate, Richard Nixon, win the general election by presenting himself as a "law and order" candidate.
Hundred Days	First hundred days of Franklin Roosevelt's presidency. During this time, Roosevelt and Congress passed an immense amount of legislation intended to help Americans during the Depression.
Hungarian Uprising	A rebellion by the Hungarians against the Russians during the 1950s. Dwight Eisenhower did not assist the Hungarians, the rebellion was crushed, and America lost credibility throughout Europe as a protector and ally.
Hutchinson, Anne	A Puritan dissenter who lived in Massachusetts Bay. Developed the philosophy of antinomianism. This philosophy threatened the church and the male-dominated society. Consequently, she was banished from the colony.
Hydrogen Bomb	Developed by America during the Cold War in an attempt to win the arms race. The H-bomb was 1000 times more powerful than the atomic bomb. Many leading scientists opposed its development.

Immigration Act of 1924	Quota system designed to limit the number of new immigrants allowed into America during the 1920s. Capped the number of new immigrants from a given country to 2% of the number of people from that country already living in the U.S. as of the 1890 census.
Impending Crisis of the South, The	Book written by Hinton Helper. Attacked the slave system on the basis that it created an economic barrier to whites; Helper was not attempting to attack racism.
Impressment	Forced military service meant to ensure the British navy had a sufficient number of sailors. Led to the War of 1812.
Incas	A powerful Indian empire in Peru. They were defeated by conquistadores led by Francisco Pizarro.
Indentured Servants	Poor English citizens who sold themselves into a seven-year period of servitude in return for passage to America. Created a larger workforce, which was necessary to support tobacco plantations.
Indian Removal Act	Law passed by Congress and signed by Andrew Jackson ordering the removal of the Cherokees from Georgia. Ignored the *Worchester v. Georgia* verdict. Led to the Trail of Tears.
Industrial Revolution	Period of immense growth in American manufacturing. Originated in 1791 when Samuel Slater built the first textile mill in New England; gained momentum after the War of 1812.

Influence of Sea Power Upon History, The	Book written by Alfred Thayer Mahan at the end of the Gilded Age. Stated that a powerful two-ocean navy was necessary for international supremacy. Britain and Germany both applied the lessons of his book in the years preceding WWI.
Initiative	Progressive Era reform that allows citizens to gather a sufficient number of signatures to place a measure on a ballot to be voted on in a future election. This process bypasses the legislature, which helped reduce the corruption in passing legislation.
Interchangeable Parts	Originally created by Eli Whitney to replace musket parts. The significance is that when these parts were produced for machines, it allowed for breakdowns to be fixed quickly and assisted the Industrial Revolution.
Internment Camps	Created following the attack on Pearl Harbor when Franklin Roosevelt signed Executive Order 9066. Forced Japanese Americans living on the west coast to leave their homes and become imprisoned.
Interstate Commerce Act / Interstate Commerce Commission	Law which created a governmental committee designed to regulate interstate commerce by railroads. Significant because it was the first committee designed for this purpose; however, the committee did not have the resources necessary to be effective.

Intolerable Acts	Laws passed by Parliament to punish colonists for the Boston Tea party. Also known as the Coercive Acts. Included the Boston Port Act which closed Boston Harbor, the removal of the Massachusetts Charter, and protection for any British official who may be blamed for the responsibility of the death of a colonist. Made the colonists fear their rights were being infringed upon.
Iran-Contra Scandal	Senior members of the Reagan administration illegally sold weapons to Iran without congressional approval. The money from these sales was then given to the Contra rebels to fight against the communist government of Nicaragua.
Iranian Hostage Crisis	During Jimmy Carter's presidency, Iranian revolutionaries broke into the American embassy in Tehran and took the American diplomats hostage for 444 days. Carter could not end the crisis. The hostages were released hours after Ronald Reagan became president.
Irreconcilables	Senators led by Henry Cabot Lodge who successfully opposed the Treaty of Versailles. The U.S. never ratified the treaty and also was not a part of the League of Nations.
Irving, Washington	Author of *The Legend of Sleepy Hollow*. This book, popular following the War of 1812, was an example of the nationalist feelings that followed the war. The book centered on American themes in New England.

Isolationism	Foreign policy that avoids alliances in an effort to avoid being pulled into wars. This policy was initiated with George Washington and continued to guide U.S. foreign policy until the Spanish-American War.
Jackson, Andrew	General in the U.S. military and president of the United States. Controversial figure who his detractors claimed governed as if he were king. Significant events during his presidency were the Nullification Crisis, Trail of Tears, and Bank War.
Jackson, Helen Hunt	Author of *A Century of Dishonor*, which describes the maltreatment of Native Americans over 100 years of history.
Jackson, Thomas "Stonewall"	Confederate general during the Civil War. Received nickname when his men stood like a stone wall during the Battle of Bull Run. This action allowed reinforcements to arrive and the Confederacy to win the battle.
Jamestown	First permanent British colony in North America. Created for the purpose of finding gold; ultimately gained wealth through the cultivation of tobacco.
Jay's Treaty	Agreement brokered by John Jay between the U.S. and Great Britain to resolve continuing issues following the American Revolution. It was undermined by Alexander Hamilton and created wider divisions between political factions, but it did lead to Pinckney's Treaty.

Jefferson, Thomas	Author of the Declaration of Independence, Anti-Federalist, Secretary of State, and President. Claimed his election was revolutionary. Purchased the Louisiana Territory. Philosophically a strict constructionist.
Jim Crow Laws	Racist laws passed in southern states to disenfranchise black voters and enforce segregation.
John Deere Plow	First steel plow. Important during the Market Revolution. Allowed western farmers to grow enough food to feed the nation.
Johnson, Andrew	President during Reconstruction. Sympathized with southern states and clashed with the Republican Congress.
Johnson Debt Default Act	Law that prohibited granting a loan to a nation that had not repaid loans to the U.S. from WWI.
Johnson, Lyndon B.	President who took office after the Kennedy assassination. Instituted the Great Society, meant to eliminate racial injustice and poverty. Escalated the Vietnam War.
Joint Stock Companies	Companies formed by groups of investors to help reduce financial risk when colonizing America. The Virginia Company created Jamestown.
Jones Act	Passed by Woodrow Wilson. Announced the intention of the U.S. to give the Philippines its independence.
Joseph, Chief	Chief of the Nez Perce. Wanted his tribe to join the Sioux during the Indian Wars of the Gilded Age.

Judicial Review	Created by the *Marbury v. Madison* case. Stated that the Supreme Court had the ability to determine which laws were unconstitutional. Expanded the power of the federal government and contradicted the Kentucky and Virginia Resolutions.
Just Say No	Advertising campaign slogan championed by first lady Nancy Reagan, to prevent drug use by children.
Kallen, Horace	Cultural pluralist who believed immigrants should retain their traditions.
Kamikaze Attacks	Suicide missions by Japanese pilots during World War II in which they would attempt to crash their planes into aircraft carriers and ships.
Kansas-Nebraska Act	A compromise devised by Stephen Douglas in response to the Gadsden Purchase. In exchange for building the transcontinental railroad through the North, the Nebraska Territory would be divided into two territories, Kansas and Nebraska. Each would apply popular sovereignty to determine if it was free or slave soil. This undermined the Missouri Compromise.
Kellogg-Briand Pact	Agreement between countries signed after WWI that they would not use war as an aggressive method to resolve disputes. A nonwar pact.
Kennan, George	Created the strategy of containment.
Kennedy, John F.	President of the U.S. Created the New Frontier, which advanced the space program. Supporter of Civil Rights. Struggled with foreign policy. Assassinated in 1963.

Kennedy, Robert	Democratic candidate for president in 1968 before being assassinated. His death led to upheaval at the 1968 Democratic Convention.
Kent State	College campus where protests against the Vietnam War occurred. The National Guard was called in to end the protests; the Guardsmen shot and killed four students.
Kentucky and Virginia Resolutions	Statements written by Thomas Jefferson and James Madison in opposition to the Alien and Sedition Acts. Argued that states had the ability to nullify a law they felt violated the Constitution.
Kesey, Ken	A writer who led a hippie group called the Merry Pranksters that played tricks on those they identified as being part of "the establishment."
Keynesian Economics	Theory that government should increase spending during times of economic distress. Used by Franklin Roosevelt during the Great Depression.
Khrushchev, Nikita	Leader of the Soviet Union during the Cold War. Removed missiles from Cuba to resolve the Cuban Missile Crisis.
King, Martin Luther, Jr.	A leader of the Civil Rights Movement. Created the Southern Christian Leadership Conference. Used a strategy of nonviolent civil disobedience.
King Phillip's War	A conflict that broke out in New England due to expansion of colonial settlement. Although Metacomet (King Phillip) was able to create inter-tribal unity, the Indians were defeated.

Kitchen Debates	Debates between Richard Nixon and Nikita Khrushchev arguing which form of economy was better, capitalist or socialist.
Knights of Labor	Union of skilled and unskilled workers led by Terence Powderly. Main goals were an eight-hour workday, an end to child labor, and a graduated income tax. Dissolved after the Haymarket Riot.
Know-Nothings	A secretive anti-immigrant, anti-Catholic political party that existed during the 1850s.
Korean War	War between the communist North Koreans (supported by China and the Soviet Union) and the democratic South Koreans (supported by the United States). It began when the North Koreans attacked across the 38th parallel in hopes of reunifying the country. U.S. military forces were led by General Douglas MacArthur and were able to drive the North Koreans back across the 38th parallel.
Ku Klux Klan (KKK)	A terrorist organization started during Reconstruction which intimidated, beat, and murdered freedmen.
L'Ouverture, Toussaint	Leader of the Haitian Revolution. This revolution helped lead to the Louisiana Purchase.
Labor Unions	An organization of employees who work together to achieve common goals such as improved pay and benefits, safer working conditions, and better working conditions. This is most commonly achieved through collective bargaining.

La Follette, Robert	Progressive Governor of Wisconsin. Due to the progressive reforms implemented by La Follette, Wisconsin gained the nickname the "laboratory of democracy."
Laird Rams	Two ships being built by an English shipbuilder for the Confederacy. The ships were meant to ram into Union ships enforcing the blockade. Abraham Lincoln threatened to invade British Canada if the ships were delivered. This threat, along with Union victories at Gettysburg and Vicksburg, influenced the British government to prevent the ships' delivery and instead purchase them for England.
Laissez-faire	To leave alone; policy by the U.S. government which allowed business almost total freedom to act without government regulation. Primarily used during the Gilded Age and the 1920s.
Land Grant	Federal land given to railroad companies for building the transcontinental railroad. Allowed the railroads to sell the land and profit.
Land Ordinance	A successful aspect of the Articles of Confederation which divided land in the Old Northwest into towns. The towns were divided into 36 parcels to be sold. Money from the sale was used to repay loans from the American Revolution. One parcel of land was set aside for the building of a school.
Landrum-Griffin Act	Law passed by President Eisenhower that weakened unions by outlawing boycotts and picketing by labor unions.

League of Nations   Originally the idea of Woodrow Wilson. An international organization created after WWI dedicated to peacefully resolve international conflict. Although it was Wilson's idea, the Irreconcilables led by Henry Cabot Lodge stopped the U.S. from joining. This greatly weakened the League.

Leary, Timothy   A Harvard psychologist who encouraged exploration with drugs.

Lecompton Constitution   Constitution written for Kansas which allowed for unrestricted slavery.

Lee, Robert E.   Confederate general during the Civil War.

Lend-Lease   Law allowed the U.S. to sell and lend weapons to nations fighting against the Axis powers during World War II.

Levittowns   Mass production of homes following WWII, leading to the expansion of the suburbs.

Lexington   Colonial arsenal. The British troops successfully defeated the colonists and captured the weapons stored there.

Liberator, The   Abolitionist newspaper edited by William Lloyd Garrison.

Lincoln, Abraham   President of the U.S. during the Civil War.

Lincoln-Douglas Debates   Series of debates between Abraham Lincoln and Stephen Douglas in the race for U.S. Senate.

Literacy Test	An example of a Jim Crow law. Required voters to pass a reading test in southern states. The purpose was to prevent freedmen from voting.
Little Bighorn, Battle of	A victory for the Plains Indians during the Indian Wars of the late 19th century. Referred to as Custer's Last Stand.
Little Rock Nine	Nine African American students who integrated Central High School in Little Rock, Arkansas. Occurred due to the *Brown v. Board* decision.
Lodge, Henry Cabot	Republican congressman who led the Irreconcilables in opposing the ratification of Treaty of Versailles and the U.S. becoming a member of the League of Nations.
London Economic Conference	Meeting of 66 countries to address the worldwide depression in 1933. The U.S. attended but did not agree to the recommendations because FDR wanted to implement an inflationary monetary policy.
Long Island, Battle of	The Continental army, led by George Washington, was defeated by the British but escaped by crossing the Delaware River. This was significant because Washington's forces were able to continue to fight and win future battles.
Loose Construction	The perspective that what the Constitution does not forbid, it allows. Supported by Alexander Hamilton.
Lost Generation	A group of authors in the 1920s who wrote about the disillusionment felt by many following WWI.

Louisiana Purchase	Acquisition of the Louisiana territory by Thomas Jefferson from the French. Gave the U.S. permanent access to the Mississippi River.
Lowell Mill	Textile mill that employed women.
Loyalty Oaths	Harry Truman ordered background checks on federal employees and insisted on oaths stating they were not members of the Communist Party.
Luther, Martin	Began the Protestant Reformation by nailing his 95 theses to a church door in Wittenberg, Germany.
Lynching	Form of terrorism and murder used by racist whites to promote white supremacy and black powerlessness. Over 3,000 lynchings of African Americans were recorded from 1882-1968.
Lyon, Mary	Founded the Mount Holyoke Seminary which was dedicated to educating women.
MacArthur, Douglas	American general in the Pacific Theater of war during WWII. Oversaw reconstruction of Japan after the war. Key general during the Korean War.
Macon's Bill No. 2	Law passed during James Madison's presidency meant to persuade Britain and France to stop attacking American ships.
Madison, James	Author of the Constitution and the Virginia Resolution. President during the War of 1812.
Mahan, Alfred Thayer	Author of *The Influence of Sea Power Upon History*. Britain and Germany applied the lessons of his book in the years preceding WWI.

Maine, The	An American battleship that was monitoring the Cuban rebellion against the Spanish. The ship blew up off the coast of Havana. Yellow journalists inaccurately blamed the Spanish and this brought the U.S. into the Spanish American War.
Maine Law of 1851	Law passed by Governor Neal Dow which enforced temperance in the state of Maine.
Malcolm X	Civil rights leader associated with militancy. Was temporarily a member of the Nation of Islam. Delivered the famous speech *The Ballot or the Bullet*.
Manchuria	Resource-rich region of China invaded by the Japanese in 1931, in violation of the Kellogg-Briand Pact.
Manhattan Project	Code name for the secret project to develop the atomic bomb. Led by J. Robert Oppenheimer.
Manifest Destiny	19th century belief that America was destined by God to control the land between the Atlantic and Pacific Oceans.
Mann, Horace	Education reformer in Massachusetts during the Reform Era. Created a longer school year, increased teachers' salaries, improved teacher training programs, and improved school facilities.
Mao Zedong	Communist ruler of China. Defeated Chiang Kai-shek and the nationalists during the Chinese Civil War.

Marbury v. Madison	Supreme Court case that created judicial review. William Marbury believed that Secretary of State James Madison should be forced to deliver a commission that would make Marbury a judge. Chief Justice John Marshall agreed that Madison's refusal to do so was illegal; however, the court could not enforce this decision based on the Judiciary Act of 1789, as it went beyond the scope of the court's constitutional power.
March on Birmingham	Civil rights protest led by Dr. Martin Luther King to expose the racism of the city of Birmingham. This was extremely dangerous due to the chief of police, Bull Connor's, reputation for violence against peaceful protesters.
March on Washington	1963 political rally in Washington, D.C. to advocate for an end to political oppression based on race and equal job opportunities for the black community. Site of the *I Have a Dream* speech.
March to the Sea	Military campaign led by General Sherman during the Civil War. During this march, Sherman burned cities to the ground, destroyed railroad lines, and disrupted the Southern economy.
Margin	A form of speculation in the stock market. Investors secured loans to buy stock with the belief that they could make a profit and pay back the loan in the future. Led to the Stock Market Crash and the Great Depression.

Market Revolution	Period of American history in the early 19th century marked by new inventions, improvements in transportation, and a larger workforce most notably women and immigrants.
Marshall, John	Committed Federalist and Chief Justice of the Supreme Court.
Marshall Plan	American program that gave money to nations of western Europe to help them rebuild after WWII in an effort to ensure these nations did not become communist. It was a key component of the containment strategy.
Massachusetts Bay	Principal colony in New England settled by the Puritans. The first governor was Jonathan Winthrop, who intended to make the colony "a city upon a hill."
Mayflower, The	Boat that the Separatists sailed on.
Mayflower Compact	Agreement made by the Separatists which stated that they would make their communal decisions through the process of majority rule; however, it was not a form of government.
McCarthy, Eugene	Democratic candidate in the primary election of 1968. Supported an end to the Vietnam War like fellow Democratic George McGovern. As a result, they split the anti-war vote; Hubert Humphrey, a pro-war Democrat, won the primary election.

McCarthy, Joseph Wisconsin senator who claimed that there were communist spies in the U.S. government. His accusations destroyed the careers and lives of many innocent Americans. Eventually censured after the Army-McCarthy hearings.

McClellan, George General in the Union Army who commanded the Army of the Potomac. Known for being overcautious and, as a result, won few battles. Fired by Abraham Lincoln twice. McClellan ran for president against Lincoln in 1864.

McCormick Reaper Farming machine created by Cyrus McCormick. Rapidly increased the rate at which crops could be harvested. Allowed the West (Midwest) to specialize in farming and feed the nation during the Market Revolution.

McCulloch v. Maryland Supreme Court case. The state of Maryland tried to eliminate a branch of the Bank of the United States by taxing it. The Supreme Court led by Chief Justice John Marshall declared this unconstitutional stating "the power to tax is the power to destroy." Also showed that the power of the state was inferior to the federal government.

McGovern, George Democratic candidate in the primary election of 1968. He supported an end to the Vietnam War like fellow Democratic Eugene McCarthy. As a result, they split the anti-war vote; Hubert Humphrey, a pro-war Democrat, won the primary election.

McKinley, William President of the U.S.; opposed the coining of silver.

McNary-Haugen Bill	Controversial bill intended to help farmers by creating a scarcity of farm products, which would drive up the cost of agricultural goods and give farmers higher profits. It was never passed into law.
Meat Inspection Act	Law passed due to the book *The Jungle* by Upton Sinclair. Mandated that meat must be inspected, and if found unsafe, condemned from being sold.
Medicaid	Program instituted by Lyndon Johnson's Great Society. It guaranteed healthcare for the poor.
Medicare	A medical insurance program for the elderly created by Lyndon Johnson. Before its passage, over 40% of Americans over 65 did not have health insurance.
Mencken, H.L.	A writer in the 1920s associated with the Lost Generation. His works attacked traditional American institutions such as marriage, Puritan values, and democracy.
Mercantilism	Economic policy by which powerful countries control colonies in order to take their resources and increase the wealth of the powerful country. In terms of the British colonies, raw materials were shipped to England, made into a finished good and sold back to the colonists in America.
Meredith, James	Forced the Kennedy administration to enforce civil rights for African Americans by being the first African American to be admitted to Ole Miss. The Kennedy administration sent 500 federal marshals to protect Meredith during registration.

Merrimack, The	Confederate ironclad ship intended to help break the Union blockade of southern ports.
Merry Pranksters	A small counterculture group led by author Ken Kesey. They traveled throughout the U.S. in a bus named Further and played pranks on "The Establishment."
Mexican Cession	The acquisition of Mexican land ceded to the United States following the Mexican War. It includes the area that now comprises these five states: California, Arizona, New Mexico, Nevada, and Utah. This additional land led to disputes in the sectional balance.
Middle Passage	The second leg of the triangle trade route, which transported African slaves to the West Indies.
Midway, Battle of	Battle during World War II in which the U.S. defeated the Japanese, ensuring that Pearl Harbor would be safe from future attacks.
Minutemen	Nickname given to colonial militia men because they could be ready to fight in a minute's notice. The minutemen prevented British troops from taking the weapons from the arsenal at Concord.
Miranda v. Arizona	Supreme Court case which determined that a person who is arrested must be informed of his or her rights.
Missions	An organized effort by the Spanish to convert Indians to Catholicism in the Americas.

Missouri Compromise	Created by Henry Clay to resolve the issue of Missouri's statehood. To maintain the sectional balance, Missouri became a slave state and Maine became a free state. To avoid future conflict, it was agreed that any territory from the Louisiana Purchase above 36°30' would be free soil and territory below would be slave territory.
Molasses Act	A tax placed on molasses the colonists were buying from the French West Indies. The purpose was to stop the trade; however, it led to colonial smuggling instead.
Monitor, The	Union ironclad ship that was designed to protect wooden naval ships trying to uphold the blockade on southern ports.
Monk, Maria	Author of *The Awful Disclosures of Maria Monk.* This book was written to foster distrust and hatred toward Catholics.
Monroe Doctrine	American policy stating that any attempts by European nations to reestablish or create new colonies in the Western Hemisphere would be viewed as an act of war. Did not dispute European countries' right to maintain the colonies they already controlled in the Western Hemisphere.
Monroe, James	President of the U.S. during the Era of Good Feelings. Created the Monroe Doctrine.

Montgomery Bus Boycott	Began when Rosa Parks refused to follow the racist policy that required her to give up her bus seat to a white person. Led to her arrest. In response, a boycott of the bus company occurred until the Supreme Court declared the policy unconstitutional.
Moral Majority	A political group made up of fundamentalist Christians. Associated with the New Right.
Mosaddegh, Mohammad	Prime Minister of Iran during the 1950s who nationalized Iran's oil. The U.S. feared that he was a communist and organized a coup to overthrow him. In his place the shah, Mohammad Reza Pahlavi, ruled as a brutal dictator.
Muckrakers	A term used to describe journalists whose written works were meant to expose corruption and inspire improvements during the Reform Era.
Muir, John	Environmentalist who believed in preservation. Created the Sierra Club and challenged other environmentalists who believed in conservation.
Mujahideen	An Afghani religious force supported by the U.S.; fought against the Russians in Afghanistan.
Munich Agreement	Pact between Great Britain, France, and Germany; allowed Germany to take control of Czechoslovakia. This was the most famous example of German appeasement leading up to WWII. British Prime Minister Neville Chamberlain mistakenly claimed that they had "guaranteed peace in our time."
Mussolini, Benito	Fascist leader of Italy during WWII. Violated the Kellogg-Briand Pact when he invaded North Africa.

Mutually Assured Destruction	A doctrine that assumed that if the U.S. and U.S.S.R. went to war, there was enough destructive power in their nuclear arsenals to destroy the world.
Mỹ Lai Massacre	During the Vietnam War, a company of American soldiers killed between 350-500 unarmed civilians in the village of Mỹ Lai. When this became public, it led to increased opposition of the Vietnam War.
Nagasaki	Japanese city where the second atomic bomb was dropped during World War II.
Napoleon	French military and political leader. Fought wars to control Europe. Sold the Louisiana Territory to the U.S.
Narrative of the Life of Frederick Douglass	Autobiographical account of Frederick Douglass's life. Illustrated the horrors of slavery.
Nasser, Gamal Abdel	Leader of Egypt. Nationalized the Suez Canal which led to the Suez Crisis in 1956.
Nation of Islam	Led by Elijah Muhammad in the 1960s. It was a group of militant black Americans who held Islamic beliefs.
National Association for the Advancement of Colored People (NAACP)	Civil rights organization founded by W.E.B. Du Bois to promote equal rights, to eradicate prejudice; to advance the interest of non-white citizens; to secure for them impartial suffrage; and to increase their opportunities to secure justice in the courts, education for children, employment according to their ability, and complete equality in the eyes of the law. Supported anti-lynching legislation.

National Labor Union (NLU)	First national labor union. Best known for advocating for an eight-hour workday. Disbanded during the panic of 1873.
National Organization for Women (NOW)	Began in 1966. Advocated for equal employment opportunities and equal pay for women. Also supported the legalization of abortion and the equal rights amendment.
National Origins Act	A U.S. law passed in the 1920s that limited the number of new immigrants from any given country to 2% of the number of people from that country living in the U.S. as of the 1890 census. The purpose of this law was to reduce the number of New Immigrants.
National Recovery Administration	A New Deal agency. The purpose was to oversee the relationship between labor and management to improve working conditions. This included fair wages and hours. The NRA was determined to be unconstitutional by the Supreme Court.
National War Labor Board	A New Deal board comprised of a group of labor and business leaders whose purpose was to settle disputes to ensure that strikes did not occur and hurt the war effort.
Nativist	A person who favored people born in America and treated immigrants with hostility. Examples include the Know Nothings and the American Protective Association.

NATO	North Atlantic Treaty Organization. Military alliance created after WWII by the U.S. and western European nations to protect from communist attacks and expansion. NATO's motto was an attack on one is an attack on all, which guaranteed that if the Soviet Union attacked one NATO country, it would have a large force to fight against.
Natural Rights	Belief spread during the Enlightenment by John Locke. Stated that people had rights that no government could take away, specifically life, liberty, and property.
Navigation Acts	Laws created by the British to enforce mercantilism. Stated that colonists could trade only with the British. Led to smuggling via the triangle trade.
Necessary and Proper Clause	Provision in Article I of the Constitution, also known as the "elastic clause." Specifies that the government can carry out actions that are necessary and proper for the functioning of the government. Used to further Alexander Hamilton's economic plans, specifically the Bank of the United States.
Neutrality Act of 1939	Act which ended the earlier arms embargo created by the Neutrality Act of 1935. Allowed the U.S. to sell weapons to belligerent nations if the purchases were paid in cash and transported by the nation purchasing the weapons.
Neutrality Acts of 1935, 1936, and 1937	A series of laws which attempted to prevent the U.S. from being drawn into WWII. These acts outlawed transactions with belligerent nations, including selling or transporting their war materials, granting loans, or traveling on their ships.

Neutrality Proclamation	Announcement by George Washington that the U.S. would not assist France in its conflict with Great Britain, thereby ignoring the Franco-American alliance.
New Deal	Plan by Franklin Roosevelt to help Americans during the Great Depression. It used Keynesian economic principles to create jobs, assist farmers, and create social welfare programs.
New England Emigrant Aid Society	Antislavery organization which helped people from New England move to Kansas in an attempt to ensure Kansas would have the votes necessary to make it a free state (due to the Kansas-Nebraska Act). This angered the pro-slavery forces which led to the Border Ruffians voting in Kansas illegally.
New Frontier	John F. Kennedy's domestic plan which included the Peace Corps and efforts to improve education and space exploration.
New Immigrants	Term given to immigrants coming from southern and eastern Europe during the Gilded Age. Primarily Polish, Italian, and Russian Jews.
New Jersey Plan	A proposal given to the Constitutional Convention which outlined a plan for government which included a unicameral legislature with equal representation from each state. Favored small states.
New Left	Activists in the 1960s and 1970s who campaigned for civil and political rights. This included counterculture groups such as the hippies and Students for a Democratic Society.

New Orleans, Battle of	Battle in which Andrew Jackson led American troops to victory over a much larger British force. The War of 1812 was over by the signing of the Treaty of Ghent; however, word had not traveled quickly enough. Though this battle had no impact on the war, it led to a feeling of pride that strengthened the nationalist spirit after the war.
New Right	Activists in the 1970s and 1980s who campaigned for political and economic conservatism. This included groups such as Focus on the Family and the Moral Majority.
Newton, Huey	Political activist who founded the Black Panther Party.
Nez Perce	Indian tribe living in Oregon. Led by Chief Joseph, who attempted to keep his people from forced relocation to a reservation.
Ngo Dinh Diem	President of South Vietnam during the Vietnam War until his assassination.
Nixon, Richard	Leading member of HUAC. President of the United States. Architect of détente. Forced to resign due to Watergate Scandal. Enacted many policies which protected the environment.
Nonimportation Agreements	Colonial boycott of British goods in response to the Stamp Act.
Non-Intercourse Act	Created by President Jefferson to replace the Embargo Act. Allowed trade with all nations except Britain and France.

Normandy, Battle of	Major battle during World War II in which 156,000 Allied troops landed on the beach in Normandy, France, and successfully defeated the Axis forces. This allowed the Allies to liberate France and defeat the Axis throughout Europe.
Northwest Ordinance	Created by Congress to encourage an orderly settlement of the Old Northwest. Territories could become states once they had a population of 60,000, and as a result of statehood, residents would have full political representation, ensuring the territories would not be treated as colonies. The ordinance also outlawed slavery in the Old Northwest.
NSC-68	A memo which stated that the U.S. could afford to quadruple military spending to combat the spread of communism.
Nueces River	River that the Mexican government considered the border between Texas and the U.S. President Polk had U.S. troops cross this river to instigate a war.
Nullification	Theory asserting that states could overrule (nullify) federal laws they felt were unconstitutional.
Nullification Crisis	Conflict between South Carolina and the federal government under President Jackson over the Tariff of Abominations. Violence was avoided by Henry Clay's Compromise Tariff of 1833.
Nuremberg Trials	Trials of Nazis following WWII.

Nye Report	Document which stated that U.S involvement in World War I was caused by businessmen who believed they could profit from the war. This report led Americans to return to isolationist policies following the war.
Office of Price Administration (OPA)	Federal agency created during WWII to prevent wartime inflation.
Ohio River Valley	Area of land which the colonists and British fought against the French for during the French and Indian War. Although the British and colonists were victorious, the colonists were prohibited from settling the land through the Proclamation of 1763.
Old Northwest	Section of land northwest of the Ohio River that the U.S. acquired from the British following the Revolutionary War.
Olive Branch Petition	A final offer of peace and loyalty by the colonists to the British after the Battle of Bunker Hill. King George refused and the American Revolution officially began.
OPEC	Organization of Petroleum Exporting Countries. Alliance of nations that produce oil to avoid price wars. Enforced an embargo on the U.S. during Jimmy Carter's presidency causing gas prices to skyrocket.
Open Door Policy	International agreement created by John Hay stating that all nations would have equal access to trade with China.

Open Shop	A business whose workers are not required to join the union. The purpose was to weaken the union by reducing membership. Businesses where union membership is required are known as closed shops.
Operation Barbarossa	Adolf Hitler's plan to attack Russia during WWII.
Operation Dixie	Attempt by labor unions to expand in the south following WWII. It was unsuccessful.
Operation Rolling Thunder	President Johnson's plan to continually drop bombs on North Vietnam in an effort to win the war. It was unsuccessful.
Oppenheimer, J. Robert	American scientist who led the effort to develop the atomic bomb at Los Alamos Laboratory in New Mexico. His work, codenamed the Manhattan Project, led to his nickname as the "father of the atomic bomb."
Orders in Council	British law that allowed the impressment of sailors and forbid foreign ships to trade with the French without first stopping at British ports to trade with the British.
Oregon Territory	Land beginning at the northern border of California and extending to 54°40'. The U.S. and England both claimed a right to areas in this territory. James Polk campaigned for president promising to fight for every inch of the Oregon Territory. However, once elected, he made a deal with the British to divide the territory at 49°40'.

Ostend Manifesto	Document that strategized a method for the U.S. to gain Cuba from the Spanish. When northerners were outraged, the attempt to acquire Cuba was abandoned.
Overspeculation	Taking out loans to invest in an opportunity hoped to generate large profits. Caused the majority of economic panics and depressions in U.S. history.
Pahlavi, Reza (Shah)	Brutal dictator who ruled Iran after the CIA helped orchestrate a coup to overthrow Mohammad Mosaddegh.
Paine, Thomas	American revolutionary who wrote the pamphlet *Common Sense.*
Palmer, A. Mitchell	Attorney General in the early 1920s. Carried out the Palmer Raids to capture and arrest suspected communists and deport them from the U.S. on the USAT *Buford,* also known as *The Soviet Ark.*
Panay, The	American ship that was sunk by the Japanese as it attempted to rescue Americans during the Rape of Nanking.
Panic of 1819	A depression caused by overspeculation. Many farmers who had their land foreclosed on blamed the Bank of the United States for their losses.
Panic of 1837	A depression caused by pet banks that were created after Andrew Jackson vetoed the recharter of the Bank of the United States. Jackson attempted to stop the depression from worsening through his Specie Circular executive order; however, it was ineffective.

Panic of 1857	Depression that affected the northern states more than the southern states. It convinced many southerners of the superiority of the southern slave system compared to the northern industrial system.
Panic of 1873	Created by overspeculation. Led to the end of the National Labor Union as desperate workers were willing to take any job offered regardless of hours.
Paris, Treaty of	Ended the American Revolution. Britain acknowledged the independence of the U.S., relinquished the Old Northwest, and promised to remove British forts on American soil.
Parks, Rosa	Activist in the Civil Rights Movement. Began the Montgomery Bus Boycott by refusing to give up her seat to a white patron.
PATCO	Professional Air Traffic Controllers Organization. Union that went on strike during Ronald Reagan's presidency. Reagan fired all of the striking workers, ending the strike and severely weakening unions.
Patent	Document given to the originator of an invention. Protects the inventor from others stealing the idea and making a profit from it.
Patronage	The political practice of rewarding political supporters with government jobs.
Paul, Alice	Women's rights advocate who fought for the Equal Rights Amendment.

Peace Corps	Program established during the Kennedy Administration. Sent volunteers to underdeveloped nations to help implement projects designed to help the poor people living in these areas.
Pearl Harbor	Location of a U.S. naval base in Hawaii. The Japanese launched a surprise attack against the U.S. while the two countries were at still at peace. The following day the U.S. joined the Allies in WWII.
Peculiar Institution	Another name for slavery.
Pendleton Act	Law meant to end patronage following the assassination of James Garfield. Stated that government jobs would be earned based on merit, as determined by the Civil Service Exam.
Peninsula Campaign	Union military campaign led by General McClellan. The purpose of the campaign was to fight from eastern Virginia to the capital of Richmond. Although McClellan won the early battles, he was later driven back by Confederate General Lee.
Penn, William	Quaker who created the colony of Pennsylvania. Known as a colony which was tolerant of different religions and treated the Indians with respect.
Pentagon Papers	A top-secret study prepared by the Department of Defense. It showed that the war in Vietnam had been unsuccessful and the government had not been honest with the American people. It was leaked by a government analyst who believed that the public should be made aware of the information.

Pequot War	Conflict between the New England colonists and the Pequot Indians in which the Pequots were killed or captured and sold into slavery in the West Indies.
Perestroika	A policy of economic restructuring implemented by Mikhail Gorbachev. Showed that the socialist economic system was being restructured and that elements of capitalism would be allowed.
Perry, Oliver Hazard	U.S. Naval commander who defeated the British in battle on Lake Erie during the War of 1812.
Pet Banks	Term for state banks created after the Bank War eliminated the Bank of the United States. Pet banks printed too much money, which led to inflation, causing the Panic of 1837.
Philadelphia Plan	A federally mandated affirmative action plan instituted under the Nixon administration. Required construction companies that had government contracts to increase the hiring of nonwhite workers.
Philippine-American War	A conflict between the U.S. and the Philippines. Filipinos believed they would receive their independence after the Spanish-American War and were angry when they became a colony of the U.S.
Pinchot, Gifford	Chief of the Forest Service during Teddy Roosevelt's presidency. He was an environmentalist who advocated conservation rather than preservation.

Pinckney's Treaty	Caused by Jay's Treaty. The Spanish misinterpreted Jay's Treaty and believed the U.S. and Britain were building a stronger relationship. As a result, Spain wanted to improve its relationship with the U.S., so granted Americans access to the Mississippi and the Port of New Orleans.
Pittsburgh Plus Pricing	Unscrupulous business practice created by steel magnates like Andrew Carnegie. Forced railroads to increase the price of shipping to southern steel companies so that when they shipped steel south, they did not have a pricing advantage.
Plains Indians	Indigenous people who lived a nomadic lifestyle on the Great Plains and hunted buffalo as their primary resource for survival. Resisted being forced from their land through a series of battles as white settlers moved further west.
Platt Amendment	Amendment the U.S. forced the Cubans to add to their constitution after achieving independence from the Spanish. It stated that the U.S could intervene to protect its interests in Cuba, that Cuba could not make treaties with other countries which might undermine Cuban independence, and that Cuba must lease Guantanamo Bay to the U.S. for use as a naval base.
Plessy v. Ferguson	Supreme Court decision stating that segregation was legal if the separate facilities were equal ("separate but equal").
Plymouth Colony	First New England colony settled by the English. The colonists were Separatists (Pilgrims) who had left England due to their conflict with the King.

Policy of Boldness President Eisenhower's foreign policy plan. The goal was more aggressive than containment. He hoped to roll back communism.

Political Machine A form of organized crime in which leaders of the political machine (bosses) found jobs and housing for immigrants, then told the immigrants how to vote. If politicians wanted to get elected, they needed to do what the political bosses told them. Business owners would have to pay the machines if they wanted politicians to grant favors or to support their ventures. This systemic corruption undermined the democratic process. The most famous political machine was Tammany Hall.

Polk, James President of the U.S. Negotiated the division of the Oregon Territory. Instigated the Mexican War by sending American troops across the Nueces River.

Poll Tax An example of a Jim Crow law. It required voters to pay a tax to vote in southern states. However, it only applied to black voters due to the grandfather clause.

Pontiac's Rebellion To protect Indian land after the French and Indian War, Chief Pontiac led an uprising attacking British forts in the Old Northwest. His rebellion was fairly successful until the British gave the Indians blankets infected with smallpox. To avoid future wars, the British instituted the Proclamation of 1763.

Pools An informal agreement between railroads to keep prices high and competition among themselves low. Greatly hurt western farmers, who were forced to pay high prices for shipping their crops.

Popé's Rebellion	Pueblo Indian uprising in the Spanish southwest, also known as the Pueblo Revolt. The Pueblos were angry because the Spanish began demanding conversion to Catholicism. The Pueblos were victorious and drove the Spanish out of their land.
Popular Sovereignty	Practice that allowed territories to choose through popular vote whether to allow slavery or free soil. This practice was used to determine the legality of slavery in the territories gained through the Mexican Cession, as well as Kansas and Nebraska following the Kansas-Nebraska Act.
Populist Party	Political party organized to support the average person, primarily farmers. Key belief was that it was necessary to have free and unlimited coinage of silver to create inflationary monetary policy, making it easier for farmers to repay their loans. The most famous populist was William Jennings Bryan.
Powderly, Terence	President of the Knights of Labor union.
Praying Towns	A rare example of English attempts to force Indian assimilation. The Puritans created towns in which they attempted to convert Indians to Christianity and give up their hunter-gatherer lifestyle. Overall this effort was unsuccessful.
Predestination	Protestant belief shared by John Calvin which held that God had predetermined who was to enter heaven and who was not.
Priming the Pump	An economic concept that requires the government to infuse money into the economy to stimulate growth. This was a key aspect of the New Deal.

Primogeniture	English custom that allowed the oldest son to inherit all his father's property.
Princeton, Battle of	George Washington led the Continental Army to victory over the British in this battle through trickery. The colonists kept their fires burning, leaving the British to believe they were staying in camp. As a result, the British were unprepared when the colonists attacked.
Privateers	Privately owned American ships that attacked British merchant ships. Privateers were allowed to keep a percentage of the spoils, giving the rest to the U.S. government for expenses during the Revolutionary War.
Proclamation of 1763	British policy enacted after Pontiac's Rebellion. Stated that the colonists could not settle west of the Appalachian Mountains. Led to resentment of the British by the colonists.
Progressive Era	Period from the 1890s through 1920. Marked by a reform movement that was successful at addressing problems of the Gilded Age such as corruption, industrialization, and urbanization.
Prohibition	The outlawing of alcohol as legislated by the Volstead Act (18th Amendment) during the 1920s. It led to a rise in organized crime and was eventually repealed.

Protestant Reformation	Religious movement begun by Martin Luther, who asserted that the Christian church needed to be reformed due to the great degree of corruption that existed. Led to a series of religious wars throughout Europe and stoked hatred between Protestants and Catholics.
Pueblo Revolt	See Popé's Rebellion.
Pullman Palace Cars	Luxury passenger cars for trains. Eugene Debs led a famous strike by Pullman Palace Car workers.
Pure Food and Drug Act	Law enacted due to experiments by Henry Wiley and his "poison squad." The experiments tested food that contained dangerous preservatives such as formaldehyde. These tests and the articles written about them led President Theodore Roosevelt to regulate food and medicine transported through interstate commerce and outlaw any form of poisonous medicine.
Puritans	Protestants who differed from the Separatists. Puritans believed the Church of England could be reformed; as a result, they did not want to separate. Puritans settled in Massachusetts Bay; their first governor was Jonathan Winthrop.
***Quarantine* Speech**	Delivered by Franklin Roosevelt. It condemned the Japanese invasion of China and stated that a Japanese embargo should be put in place. Roosevelt's ideas were not readily accepted.
Quartering Act	A British law stating that colonists had to provide housing for British soldiers.

Quebec Act	Gave French citizens in British Canada religious freedom and instituted the traditional French judicial system in Canada. Also allowed the French to access the Ohio River Valley.
Radical Republicans	Republican party faction whose members advocated for full emancipation and civil rights for freedmen after the Civil War. Influential in the passing of the 14th Amendment.
Radical Whigs	British thinkers who believed there was a threat that the government would take away their rights as Englishmen.
Rape of Nanking	After the Japanese defeated the Chinese at Nanking in 1937, the Japanese soldiers brutalized and killed Chinese civilians.
Reagan, Nancy	First lady, wife of President Ronald Reagan. Known for her involvement in the "Just Say No" anti-drug campaign.
Reagan, Ronald	President during the 1980s who sought to improve the economy through a supply-side economic policy and the reduction of government regulations. Reagan successfully ended the Iran Hostage Crisis, but later faced scrutiny during the Iran-Contra Scandal hearings. He was also famous for using fierce anti-Communist rhetoric and for dramatically increasing military spending.
Reaganomics	Supply-side economic policy advanced by the Reagan Administration. The plan included tax cuts and a reduction of governmental programs and regulations on businesses.

Rebates	A deduction from the amount meant to be paid. Railroads would give large shippers secret rebates to ensure that they did not transport goods through competing railroads. This led to small farmers paying larger amounts to make up for the lower price given to the large shippers.
Recall	Progressive Era reform that allows citizens to remove a politician from office before the end of an elected term. This is done through a popular vote. This was an important democratic advancement as it allowed for timely removal of corrupt politicians.
Reciprocal Trade Agreements	Instituted during Franklin Roosevelt's presidency, these agreements allowed the president to lower tariffs with trading partners if foreign nations agreed to lower tariffs on U.S. goods.
Reconquista	A series of military campaigns by Christian kingdoms, similar to the Crusades, to regain territory in Spain which was being controlled by the Moors (Muslims from North Africa). It led to a desire to spread Christianity.
Reconstruction	Historical era following the Civil War. Proposed improvements were intended to help the freedmen, but little progress was made and the South continued in much the same manner it did before the war. Ended through the Compromise of 1877.
Reconstruction Amendments	Refers to the 13th, 14th, and 15th Amendments to the Constitution.

Reconstruction Finance Corporation	Government agency created by the Hoover Administration. It allocated loans to businesses in an effort to reduce the problems of the Great Depression. It was unsuccessful.
Red Army	The army and air force of the U.S.S.R., established after the Bolshevik Revolution in 1917.
Red Scare	Occurred in the 1920s and the 1950s. It was a period of hysteria in which Americans feared that communism would come to America.
Redcoats	Term for British troops during the American Revolution, so named for the color of their uniforms.
Redeemer Governments	Southern state governments during the Reconstruction period that enacted legislation to restrict the rights and opportunities of the freedmen.
Referendum	Progressive Era reform that allows the electorate to vote directly on a ballot measure. This process bypasses the legislature, and helped reduce the corruption in passing legislation.
Reform Era	Period from 1890-1920. It was noted for a reduction in government corruption, an expansion of democratic practices, and a movement to fix the problems of society.
Reformers	People devoted to improving society through changing the status quo.

Republican Motherhood	The role expected of women following the American Revolution. Women were expected to stay in the home and teach their children civic virtue so they could become responsible citizens who would support democracy.
Republicanism	Belief that in a just government the power flowed up from the people to their leaders. This belief supported the idea that the government should carry out the will of the people.
Revolution of 1800	Term Thomas Jefferson gave to his electoral victory. He believed it was revolutionary due to the peaceful transition of power from one political party to another.
Revolutionary War	War between American colonists and the British. The war was a result of colonial dissatisfaction with British rule which led to the colonists declaring their independence.
Rhineland	Area of land that became a demilitarized zone through a provision of the Treaty of Versailles. In 1936 German troops marched into the Rhineland and regained control of the area. This allowed the Germans to take additional land in Eastern Europe.
Riis, Jacob	Photojournalist and muckraker whose book *How the Other Half Lives* documented the deplorable living conditions in the slums of large cities.
Robber Barons	Big business owners during the Gilded Age. Known for paying low wages and eliminating competition so they could create monopolies. Once they had a monopoly, they could charge high prices.

Rockefeller, John D.	Strongest example of a robber baron. Rockefeller used horizontal integration to gain control of 95% of all oil in the United States.
Roe v. Wade	Supreme Court case that determined abortion was a privacy issue, and as a result decided that states could not outlaw it.
Rolfe, John	Colonist who realized the soil in Virginia would allow for the cultivation of tobacco.
Roll Back	Strategy of removing communist governments from Soviet satellite nations. More aggressive than containment, largely unsuccessful.
Rome-Berlin Axis	Alliance between Italy and Germany forged in 1936.
Rommel, Erwin	German general nicknamed the Desert Fox who led German and Italian troops in the battle of Northern Africa during World War II. His forces were defeated in the Battle of El Alamein.
Roosevelt Corollary	An addition to the Monroe Doctrine made by Theodore Roosevelt. It stated that the U.S. would intervene to ensure Latin American nations repaid debts to European creditors. This policy was created to prevent European nations from intervening in countries located in the Western Hemisphere.
Roosevelt, Franklin Delano	President of the U.S. during the Great Depression and World War II. Created the New Deal.

Roosevelt, Theodore (Teddy)	President known for being a reformer. Roosevelt created the Square Deal, which was meant to control corporations, offer consumers protection, and promote conservation. He also used a "big stick" foreign policy to influence other nations.
Root-Takahira Agreement	Agreement between the U.S. and Japan in which Japan agreed to accept America's annexation of Hawaii and control of the Philippines; the U.S. agreed to accept Japan's control of Korea and dominance of Manchuria; both nations agreed to respect the Open Door policy in China.
Rosenberg, Julius and Ethel	American citizens who transmitted nuclear secrets to the Soviet Union. They were convicted of espionage in 1951 and executed in 1953.
Royal African Company	A trading company that had a monopoly on the sale of slaves. This led to slaves being very expensive. As a result, the English colonies used indentured servants as a labor force until Bacon's Rebellion occurred and the Royal African Company lost its monopoly.
Royal Colony	A colony whose governor and other officials are selected by the king.
Rush-Bagot Agreement	An agreement made following the War of 1812 to reduce armaments on the Great Lakes in an effort to diminish the likelihood of an unintended war.

Sacco and Vanzetti   Italian immigrants who were accused of murdering a paymaster during the Red Scare of the 1920s. Because they were immigrants and anarchists, their treatment during the trial was controversial; a contention exists that they were not given a fair trial. They were found guilty and executed.

SALT   Strategic Arms Limitation Talks. Initiated by Richard Nixon with the Soviet Union. This led to limiting the number of nuclear weapons both countries developed. Serves as an example of détente.

SALT II   Agreement signed by Jimmy Carter and Leonid Brezhnev which offered guidelines and limits on the production of nuclear weapons. This agreement was a failure since in never went into effect due to the Soviet invasion of Afghanistan.

Salutary Neglect   Period during which the British government did not strictly enforce its laws over the American colonies.

San Jacinto, Battle of   Final battle of the Texas Revolution. Three weeks later Santa Anna signed the peace treaty which gave Texas independence.

Sanger, Margaret   American birth control activist who was arrested in 1916 for opening a family planning clinic in Brooklyn (the first in the United States).

Saratoga, Battle of   First major victory for the colonists during the Revolutionary War. Following the Battle of Saratoga, the French joined the U.S. in the war effort through the Franco-American Alliance.

Satellite	A country of eastern Europe that appeared to be independent but was under the political and economic influence of the Soviet Union.
Schlafly, Phyllis	A conservative female activist during the 1970s. She effectively lobbied against the passage of the ERA, believing that women would be in peril if men were not expected to provide for them.
Scopes, John	Substitute teacher who taught about evolution.
Scopes Monkey Trial	Famous trial which occurred in Tennessee in the 1920s. The state had outlawed the teaching of evolution. John Scopes ignored the law and was put on trial. This case illustrated the conflict between modernity/science and tradition.
Scott, Dred	Slave who sued for his freedom, arguing that because he lived in territory designated as free soil, he should be free. In *Dred Scott v. Sanford,* the Supreme Court ruled against him, stating that because he was not a citizen, he did not have the right to a trial; they also ruled that slaves were property, so according to the Fifth Amendment, they could be taken anywhere and the government could not take them away from their owners.
Second Continental Congress	Gathering of delegates from all 13 colonies. Appealed to the king to repeal acts, wanted to avoid war but prepared for it by organizing an army and naming George Washington its principal general.

Second Front	An attack by the United States against the Axis in western Europe. Franklin Roosevelt had promised Joseph Stalin that he would open a second front; however, this promise was ignored and U.S. troops attacked through the soft underbelly of Italy. This led to more Russian deaths, which made Stalin feel betrayed. Eventually, the United States did open a second front in Europe during the Invasion of Normandy. This took pressure off the Russians by dividing the German forces.
Second Great Awakening	A Protestant religious movement which began in the early 1800s. It was led by circuit riders like Charles Grandison Finney and Peter Cartwright. Their message of achieving salvation through good works led to the reform movement.
Sectional Balance	The ratio of slave states to free states, important because neither side wanted the other to have an advantage. The first major issue regarding the sectional balance, the admission of Missouri as a state, was resolved by maintaining equal numbers through the Missouri Compromise. However, as more western states were added, the sectional balance continued to be a source of conflict.
Security Exchange Commission (SEC)	New Deal agency created to prevent investment fraud.
Segregation	Separation of the races, which led to the creation of separate facilities. This practice was originally deemed constitutional through the Supreme Court case *Plessy v. Ferguson*. It was later overturned through the *Brown v. Board of Education* decision.

Senatorial Balance	The ratio of senators from slave states to free soil states.
Seneca Falls Convention	Meeting led by Elizabeth Cady Stanton and Susan B. Anthony which formally launched the women's suffrage movement. The famous document *The Declaration of Rights and Sentiments,* insisting on equal rights for women, was read at the convention.
Separate But Equal	Policy of segregation upheld by *Plessy v. Ferguson,* stating that segregation was constitutional if equal facilities were provided to African Americans. Although equal facilities were mandated, the facilities provided to African Americans were starkly inferior to those provided to whites.
Separation of Powers	Concept that defines the powers of each branch of the U.S. government. A system of checks and balances was implemented to ensure no single branch became too powerful.
Separatists	English Protestants who rejected the Church of England. One group of Separatists, the Pilgrims, left for Holland and eventually traveled to Plymouth aboard the Mayflower.
Sepúlveda, Juan Ginés de	Spanish theologian who advocated for the enslavement of Latin American Indians.
Serra, Junipero, Fr.	Spanish priest who organized a chain of missions on the coast of California to convert the indigenous people to Catholicism.

Settlement House

A house in which middle-class women helped poor immigrants adjust to life in America. This was most notable during the Gilded Age. The most famous was the Hull House, established by Jane Addams. At settlement houses, immigrants could learn English, and have access to childcare and healthcare.

Shame of the Cities, The

Book written by muckraker Lincoln Steffens. Its purpose was to examine the corruption occurring in cities and encourage residents to become more active in electing moral leaders.

Sharecroppers

Freedman who, after the Civil War, were forced to work on land owned by white men for a small share of the crops they raised. This system arose because of the black codes, which outlawed ownership of land by blacks in southern states. It created an economic system in the south similar to slavery.

Shays' Rebellion

A farmers' rebellion led by Daniel Shays against the state government of Massachusetts. The farmers, in debt after the Revolutionary War, sought help from the state when banks began foreclosing on their farms. When assistance was denied, the farmers rebelled. The rebellion was eventually put down, but it caused concern among the wealthy that future rebellions could threaten their prosperity. They determined a stronger central government was needed to crush future rebellions; this led to the Constitutional Convention.

Sherman Antitrust Act	The first law passed by the federal government to prevent trusts and increase competition. However, the law was vague and the courts used the legislation to weaken unions instead.
Sherman, William Tecumseh	A general in the Union Army. Led the March to the Sea which involved the tactics of fighting a total war. He also burned Atlanta and several other southern cities to the ground.
Sherman's March to the Sea	The route Sherman followed on his way to Atlanta.
Silent Spring	Book by Rachel Carson explaining the hazards of using pesticides (e.g., DDT) on the environment. Helped initiate the environmentalist movement.
Sinclair, Upton	Muckraker who wrote *The Jungle*. His book described the terrible conditions of the meat packing plants and helped instigate the creation of the Meat Inspection Act.
Sinners in the Hands of an Angry God	Sermon given by Jonathan Edwards in which he warned that if individuals were sinners, they would face an eternity of fire and brimstone.
Sioux	Indian tribe that lived nomadically on the Great Plains. They fought to remain on their land and avoid being put on reservations. Conflicts included the Sand Creek Massacre, Fetterman's Massacre, the Battle of Wounded Knee, and the Battle of Little Bighorn.

Sit-In Movement An economic nonviolent form of protest against segregation that began at a lunch counter at Woolworth's in South Carolina. When protesters, who were black, sat down at a lunch counter and were denied service, they refused to move until they were served. This movement spread across the country.

Slater, Samuel A British citizen who was the first to begin building textile machines in the U.S. He is credited as being the father of the American Industrial Revolution.

Smallpox Deadly disease transferred from the Spanish to the Indians of Latin America. The high number of deaths that resulted was a key reason the Aztec and Inca empires were defeated by the conquistadores.

Smith, John Early governor of Jamestown. Saved the colony by establishing the rule "he who will not work, shall not eat."

Smith-Connally Anti-Strike Act An American law passed during WWII, intended to prevent strikes from slowing down production of weapons during wartime.

SNCC Student Nonviolent Coordinating Committee. Began when college students were inspired by the lunch counter sit-ins and began to participate in them. Members also participated in Freedom Rides and the Voter Registration Project. The SNCC grew more radical when Stokely Carmichael became the leader and advocated for Black Power.

Social Darwinism

Idea advanced by Henry Spencer. Similar to the theory of evolution (in which the species most able to adapt are the ones that survive and excel), social Darwinism holds that the most able humans are the ones who become the wealthiest and most powerful. This theory ignores the advantages that some are born with and the racism and systemic poverty that prevent others from gaining wealth and power.

Social Gospel

Religious movement that arose near the end of the Gilded Age and advocated for applying Christian teachings to social problems. This contradicted Social Darwinists and was reflected in many reforms that occurred in the 1900s.

Social Security

Federal program enacted in 1935 to provide Americans over the age of 65 with monthly payments from the government to help ensure they did not become impoverished in old age.

Soft Underbelly

Term for the location of an American attack in Europe by going through vulnerable Italy. The attack did not fulfill the American promise to open up a second front in Europe, which would have relieved pressure on the Russian army. As a result, Joseph Stalin felt betrayed.

Soil Conservation Act

New Deal policy which paid farmers to plant crops that would restore nutrients to the soil. This law served as a replacement for the Agricultural Adjustment Act which was found unconstitutional.

Sons of Liberty	An organization led by Sam Adams which attacked tax collectors that tried to enforce the Stamp Act. The Sons of Liberty were also the perpetrators of the Boston Tea Party.
South Carolina Exposition	A document anonymously written by John C. Calhoun (Andrew Jackson's vice president) which challenged the Tariff of Abominations.
Southern Christian Leadership Conference (SCLC)	A civil rights organization founded by Martin Luther King. This organization followed nonviolent civil disobedience practices to demand equal rights for African Americans.
Southern Strategy	Richard Nixon's campaign plan. Targeted southern states, which had a growing population following WWII, by appealing to racism against African Americans.
Spanish Civil War	This war began in 1936 and forecasted fascist aggression in Europe. General Francisco Franco led a fascist overthrow of the Republican government in Spain, with assistance from fascist nations like Germany and Italy. Western democracies did not support the democratic government of Republican Spain, and as a result, the fascists won.
Spanish-American War	Began in 1898 when the USS Maine blew up off the coast of Havana. Yellow journalists wrote articles claiming the Spanish were to blame. The U.S. went to war and defeated the Spanish. As a result, the U.S. gained several Spanish colonies in the Pacific, including Guam, Wake, and the Philippines. The U.S. also gained control of Puerto Rico and had indirect control of Cuba, both in the Caribbean.

SPARS	The women's branch of the Coast Guard during World War II. Allowed women to work at shore stations in jobs men had held, which released the men to be on ships for sea duty.
Special Field Order No. 15	An order given by General Sherman stating that 400,000 acres of Confederate land should be redistributed to freedmen in 40-acre parcels.
Spoils System	Synonym of patronage, but the term is used primarily to identify the cronyism of Andrew Jackson's presidency. It refers to the appointment to a government job as a reward for giving support to a political candidate.
Spot Resolutions	A request made by Abraham Lincoln asking President Polk to provide evidence of the exact spot blood was shed on American soil. This request was made because Polk alleged that American troops had died on American soil. The truth was that they had died on disputed territory.
Square Deal	Policy enacted by President Theodore Roosevelt meant to control corporations, offer consumers protection, and promote conservation.
Stagflation	A combination of the words "stagnant" and "inflation," used to describe an economic period in Richard Nixon's presidency. It is characterized by high unemployment and the rising costs of goods.

Stalin, Joseph	Leader of Russia during World War II. Originally created an alliance with the German government through the Hitler-Stalin Pact. However, when Germany invaded Russia, Stalin joined the Allies. Stalin served as leader of the Soviet Union through the early years of the Cold War.
Stalwarts	Term given to a faction of the Republican Party during the Gilded Age. The most famous stalwart was Roscoe Conkling. An aggrieved Stalwart (Charles Guiteau) assassinated President James Garfield, a member of the Half-Breed faction. This led to the presidency of Chester A. Arthur and the passage of the Pendleton Act.
Stamp Act	A direct tax on printed materials in the colonies. Colonists felt that a direct tax should not be levied on their goods unless they had representation in Parliament to speak and vote on their behalf. As a result, colonists resisted the tax and it was repealed.
Stamp Act Congress	A gathering of several leaders from the colonies to organize against the passage of the Stamp Act. The congress formulated a list of grievances against the British government and created the nonimportation agreements.
Standard Oil Company	John D. Rockefeller's oil company. He used horizontal integration to eliminate competition and as a result controlled 95% of all oil in the U.S.
Stanton, Elizabeth Cady	A women's rights activist during the Reform Era. She read the *Declaration of Rights and Sentiments* at the Seneca Falls Convention.

Star Wars	Also known as the Strategic Defense Initiative. The program was championed by President Ronald Reagan. The goal was to create a missile shield that was partially located in space to stop missiles launched at the U.S. by the Soviet Union. It was not implemented.
Steffens, Lincoln	Muckraker author of *The Shame of the Cities,* which examined urban corruption and advocated for city dwellers to become more active in electing moral leaders.
Stimson Doctrine	A policy in response to Japan's acquisition of Manchuria by force. The U.S. stated it did not recognize any territorial changes acquired by force. However, the U.S. did not act in any way to prevent the Japanese from maintaining control of Manchuria. As a result, the Japanese continued to control a large and resource-rich area of China.
Stock Market Crash	On Black Tuesday in 1929, the stock market dropped dramatically, and worried investors began to sell their stock. This was especially problematic because many investors had purchased their stock on margin, so they could not repay the bank loans they had taken out.
Stock Watering	Method used by Jay Gould to artificially inflate the price of his railroad stock.
Stowe, Harriet Beecher	Author of the book *Uncle Tom's Cabin,* which illustrated the horrors of slavery.

Strict Construction A literal interpretation of the Constitution. Thomas Jefferson was a strict constructionist who believed that if the Constitution did not specifically state the government had the authority to carry out an act, then it could not carry out that act; instead, according to the 10th Amendment, only the states could. He used this logic when arguing against the Bank of the United States.

Sudetenland Area of land inhabited by Germans that became part of Czechoslovakia following World War I. After taking control of Austria, Hitler met with Chamberlain and gained Britain's acceptance of German control of this land through the Munich Agreement. Shortly thereafter, Germany invaded Czechoslovakia.

Suez Crisis Occurred shortly after Gamal Abdul Nasser, the leader of Egypt, nationalized the Suez Canal. Israel, France, and Britain attacked Egypt. However, the U.S. would not provide the three nations with oil as they had expected. As a result, the attacks were over shortly and Egypt maintained control of the canal.

Suffrage The legal right to vote. Often associated with women's suffrage during the Reform Era.

Sugar Act An indirect tax created to increase revenue for the British government as a replacement for the Molasses Act. Disliked by the colonists but not fiercely opposed like the Stamp Act would be later.

Summer of Love In 1967 upwards of 100,000 people moved to the Haight-Ashbury neighborhood of San Francisco to promote the hippie lifestyle.

Sumner, Charles	Massachusetts Senator whose speech, *The Crimes Against Kansas*, angered South Carolina congressman Preston Brooks so much that Brooks beat Sumner with his cane in the Senate chamber.
Supply-Side Economics	Policy of the Reagan Administration to provide tax cuts, reduce governmental programs, and lessen regulations on businesses.
Taft, William H.	President of the United States. Initially he was supported by former president Teddy Roosevelt; however, Taft's unrestricted trustbusting and firing of Gifford Pinchot angered Roosevelt. Taft followed a foreign policy of dollar diplomacy.
Taft-Hartley Bill	Law passed by a Republican-dominated Congress (over President Truman's veto) which outlawed closed shops and forced union leaders to take noncommunist oaths.
Talleyrand, Charles-Maurice de	French Foreign Minister during the XYZ Affair.
Tallmadge Amendment	Amendment added to the bill for Missouri's admission to the Union. If passed, slaves already in Missouri would remain slaves, but no new slaves could be brought into the state and the children of slaves would be free. As a result, within one generation, Missouri would become a free state, upsetting the sectional balance. The bill passed the House but not the Senate; as a result, the Missouri Compromise was established.

Tammany Hall	Political machine in New York, most famously run by Boss Tweed.
Tarbell, Ida	Muckraker who wrote *The History of the Standard Oil Company,* which was the first example of investigative journalism. In it she attacked the business practices of John. D. Rockefeller.
Tariff of 1816	The first protective tariff created by the American government. It protected the fledgling American factories that had started to grow during the War of 1812.
Tariff of 1828	Also known as the Tariff of Abominations. It was passed at the end of John Quincy Adam's presidency and favored northern industrial states. The residents and legislature of South Carolina were exceptionally upset and this led to the Nullification Crisis.
Tariff of Abominations	See Tariff of 1828.
Teapot Dome Scandal	Occurred in the early 1920s during President Harding's administration. The Secretary of the Interior, Albert Fall, secretly and illegally leased oil to private oil companies so that he could profit. This oil was meant for the U.S. Navy.
Teller Amendment	An amendment created during the Spanish–American War. It stated that the United States would allow Cuba to be free after the Spanish were defeated.

Temperance	Drinking moderately or abstaining from alcohol. Part of the reform movement in the first half of the 19th century. Connected closely with women's rights as husbands would get drunk, gamble, and cavort with prostitutes, which led to economic distress, the spread of disease, and physical abuse of their wives when they returned home.
Ten Nights in a Bar-Room	Novel written by T.S. Arthur to illustrate the dangers of alcohol and promote temperance.
Tennessee Valley Authority (TVA)	Project initiated by the New Deal to bring electricity to poor areas in rural Tennessee. Once the government realized the cost of producing electricity, it reformed the way energy prices were set by private companies.
Texas Revolution	Rebellion of Americans living in Texas against the Mexican government. The Americans defeated the Mexican army, and Texas gained its independence from Mexico.
Three Sisters Farming	Farming method practiced by Indians in the Americas. It combined the cultivation of corn, beans, and squash. By improving their farming methods, Indians were able to create larger societies.
Three-Fifths Compromise	Stated that each slave should count as three-fifths of a person to determine a state's population for representation in the House of Representatives. The purpose was to ensure that neither the North nor the South would have a significant advantage in the balance of political representatives.

Tilden, Samuel　Democratic candidate for president. During the election, the results of three southern states were disputed. Instead of recounting, a compromise occurred. Republican candidate Rutherford B. Hayes became president; in return, Republicans agreed to remove troops from the South. This ended Reconstruction.

Till, Emmett　A 14-year-old African-American boy from Chicago who was murdered while visiting his relatives in Mississippi. He was lynched for offending a white woman while in a store. Till's mother held an open casket funeral to display his mutilated face to ensure the racism and brutality of his death were exposed.

Title IX　Provision of the 1972 Educational Amendments that prohibited gender-based discrimination in schools and created opportunities for women to participate in sports.

Total War　Style of war employed by General Sherman on his March to the Sea. He burned cities to the ground and destroyed everything in his path, including railroads and food supplies, to destroy Confederate morale.

Totalitarianism　A form of government that allows the leader of a nation to have complete control over all aspects of its citizens' lives.

Town Hall Meeting　Meetings that occurred in the New England colonies to address issues facing the village. At these meetings, all male landowners were allowed to vote.

Townshend Act	A small indirect tax imposed by the British on several goods. This act angered the colonists because the money that was raised was used to pay the royal governor's salary, which reduced their influence over him. Prior to this tax, the colonial legislature had the ability to influence the governor through the "power of the purse," which meant they had been in charge of his salary.
Trail of Tears	An effect of the Indian Removal Act. It refers to the forced relocation of Native American tribes. In 1838, the U.S. military forced the Cherokees to walk from Georgia to Oklahoma (known as Indian Territory). Between one-fourth and one-third of the Cherokees died along the way due to inadequate nutrition and brutal environmental conditions.
Transatlantic Trade Routes	Shipping routes across the Atlantic during the colonial period. The British expected the routes to allow colonial ships to travel only to Britain; however, other trade routes, such as the triangle trade, were developed.
Transportation Revolution	Occurred during the Market Revolution; refers to the creation of roads, canals, and railroads to allow for the shipment of goods between the North, South, and West. It enabled each region to specialize in one major industry.

Trent **Affair**	During the Civil War, a Union warship stopped a British mail ship (the *Trent*) and apprehended two southern diplomats onboard who had planned to request assistance from England for the Confederacy. The British were offended and demanded the release of the diplomats and an apology from President Lincoln. To keep England from supporting the Confederacy, Lincoln met both demands.
Trenton, Battle of	Battle in which George Washington was able to cross the Delaware River and defeat the Hessians, who were not expecting an attack.
Triangle Shirtwaist Factory Fire	A fire that occurred in a garment factory in New York. Due to a lack of fire safety precautions, 146 workers were killed; the majority were young female immigrants. The deaths led to protests, and the city government of New York passed legislation to improve safety in factories.
Triangle Trade	A trade route with three segments. Ships left New England with rum and arrived in West Africa to trade the rum for slaves. The ships then traveled to the Caribbean to trade the slaves for molasses. On the final leg of the journey, the ships returned to New England, where the molasses was made into rum. Because the colonists did not want to pay taxes on the goods they were trading to the British, they smuggled them instead, creating tension between the two groups.

Trickle-Down Economics	Policy used by the Reagan Administration. The plan included tax cuts and a reduction of governmental programs and regulations on businesses. Sometimes referred to as supply-side economics.
Tripartite Pact	A pact signed by Germany, Italy, and Japan which created the alliance of the Axis Powers during WWII. They agreed to fight together against any nation that attacked a country in their alliance.
Triple Entente	Name given to the alliance of France, Britain, and Russia during World War I.
Tripolitan War	A war that took place during Thomas Jefferson's presidency. Jefferson refused to pay tribute in return for American merchant ships' ability to sail without threat of attack through the Mediterranean Sea. The United States was victorious.
Truman Doctrine	Truman's foreign policy implemented to prevent the Soviet Union from expanding, promising military aid to any nation resisting communism. The earliest implementation was in Greece and Turkey.
Truman, Harry	President of the United States after Franklin Roosevelt's death. Responsible for the decision to drop the atomic bomb on Japan. His domestic policy, the Fair Deal, attempted to advance civil rights and assist the poor. Because Truman had desegregated the military, southern Democrats (known as Dixiecrats) did not support his policies. As a result, few of Truman's goals were met.
Trust	Another term for monopoly. A business becomes a trust by eliminating the competition.

Turner, Frederick Jackson	American historian who wrote the *Frontier Thesis*, which argued that the western region of the United States had been filled to capacity and there was nowhere left to expand. Turner believed that this would create economic problems which would ultimately threaten American democracy.
Turnpike	A privately built road which charged a toll for its use. Turnpikes improved transportation and were an early improvement during the Transportation Revolution.
Tuskegee Institute	An industrial school that taught skills to African Americans to help them achieve economic success. It was led by Booker T. Washington.
Twain, Mark	American author and satirist. Coined the phrase "the gilded age."
Tyler, John	President of the U.S. after the death of William Henry Harrison. Known for creating the joint resolution that allowed Texas to be annexed with a simple majority rather than the Constitutional requirement of a two-thirds majority.
U-Boats	German submarines used during World War I and World War II.
Uncle Tom's Cabin	Book written by abolitionist Harriet Beecher Stowe. This fictional account illustrated the horrors of slavery, particularly the anguish that occurred when family members were sold to different masters.

Underwood Tariff	Lowered the tariff on goods imported to America from 40%, as established by the Payne-Aldrich tariff, to 25%.
Unicameral Legislature	Style of legislature proposed in the New Jersey Plan, which would have had one chamber of congress.
Union	The northern states which fought against the Confederacy during the Civil War.
Union League	An African-American organization created during Reconstruction to help educate freedmen on the political process to increase their civic engagement. It also organized the building of churches, schools, and black militias for protection against racist threats.
Union Pacific Railroad Company	A railroad company which was involved in building the transcontinental railroad from the east.
Unions	Organized associations of workers who combined their resources to improve their working conditions. Also referred to as labor unions.
United Nations	An international organization created after WWII to resolve international conflicts. Similar in many ways to the League of Nations.
Universal Manhood Suffrage	The right of all white men 21 or older to vote. Created during the Market Revolution. Prior to this, a man had to also own land to vote; however, since such a large number of men became factory workers, they no longer owned land. By allowing them to vote, the possibility of conflict between the classes was diminished.

Utopian Communities	Communities organized in the wilderness during the Reform era, with the goal of escaping the vices of cities and establishing a separate, perfect society.
Valcour Island, Battle of	Battle on Lake Champlain during the Revolutionary War. Colonial forces were able to stall the British advance and prolong the battle. After the British eventually won, they chose to return to the comfort of their forts in Canada instead of remaining in New York for the winter. As a result, the British lost control of the territory they had won, and they had to attempt to regain control of it in the spring.
Valley Forge	Encampment for George Washington's soldiers during the winter of 1777-1778. The soldiers did not have adequate food, clothing, or shelter, and 2,500 died. Although there were desertions, the majority of men stayed loyal to Washington.
Van Buren, Martin	President of the United States. Failed to improve the economic condition of the nation during the Panic of 1837.
Vanderbilt, Cornelius	American businessman who grew wealthy through his railroads.
V-E Day	The day the Allies defeated the Axis power in Europe. Short for Victory in Europe Day.
Versailles, Treaty of	Peace treaty that ended WWI in 1919. The conditions demanded that the Germans take the blame for the outbreak of the war and pay reparations. It also demanded that Germany disarm and concede some of its territorial possessions.

Vertical Integration	A form of monopoly in which a single company owns all aspects of production. Andrew Carnegie's control of iron ore mines, steamships, and railroads ensured that he did not have to pay another business to manufacture steel.
Veterans Administration (VA)	Governmental agency that provided low-interest loans to veterans following WWII.
Vicksburg, Siege of	The Union Army surrounded the city of Vicksburg waiting for the Confederate soldiers to fight. After two months when the Battle of Vicksburg occurred, the Union defeated the Confederacy, gained control of Mississippi, and more importantly, controlled the Mississippi River.
Vietnam War	War between the South and North Vietnamese. U.S. troops fought on the side of South Vietnam to contain communism.
Vietnamization	Nixon's foreign policy of removing over 500,000 soldiers from Vietnam during the Vietnam War. The purpose was to make the South Vietnamese take more control of fighting against the communist forces of North Vietnam.
Virginia Plan	A proposal given to the Constitutional Convention outlining a plan for government which included a bicameral legislature with representation based on population. Favored large states.
V-J Day	The day the Allied forces achieved victory in the Pacific Theater during World War II. Short for Victory Over Japan Day.

Volstead Act	Another name for the 18th Amendment; prohibited the manufacture, transportation, or sale of alcohol.
Von Steuben, Baron	Prussian military officer who assisted the colonists during the American Revolution. Credited with organizing and training the colonial army to become an effective fighting force.
Voter Education Project	Raised money and helped orchestrate a process in which civil rights leaders would travel to the South in an effort to register African Americans to vote.
Voting Rights Act of 1965	A law created by President Johnson forbidding racial discrimination in voting such as the poll tax or the literacy test.
Voyageurs	French colonists who traded furs by canoe. They maintained cooperative relationships with the Indians they encountered and through their trade assimilated the Indians.
WAACS	The women's branch of the Army during World War II. This allowed women to work in jobs men had held and released the men to fight in the war.
Wabash, St. Louis & Pacific Railway Co. v. Illinois	Supreme Court case that determined states could not make laws regulating railroads if the railroads were involved in interstate commerce.
Wade-Davis Bill	A bill proposed by Radical Republicans in response to President Lincoln's 10% Plan for Reconstruction. It called for a majority of residents in Confederate states to pledge loyalty to the Union. Although this bill passed the House and the Senate, Lincoln pocket vetoed the bill.

Wagner Act	Also known as the National Labor Relations Act. Passed during the Great Depression, this law guarantees private-sector workers the right to unionize, collectively bargain, and strike.
Walker, David	Abolitionist and author of *An Appeal to the Colored Citizens of the World.*
Walker, William	American who led his private military into Nicaragua with the goal of creating American colonies which would allow slavery to exist.
Wallace, George	Governor of Alabama who supported segregation during the Civil Rights Movement.
War of 1812	War between the U.S. and the British (1812-1815). Britain was not respecting America's right to trade freely (freedom of the seas) and was also impressing American sailors into service. The war could be considered a draw since neither country gained any territory in the peace treaty, the Treaty of Ghent. However, there were positive outcomes for the United States, as nationalism increased and the U.S. economy became more self-sufficient.
War on Poverty	The unofficial name for President Johnson's domestic policy agenda (The Great Society) meant to end poverty in the U.S. Created Job Corps, Head Start, Medicare, Medicaid, and Food Stamps. This program was very costly, especially when combined with the cost of the ongoing Vietnam War.

War Production Board	Governmental agency that oversaw the transformation of factories from producing peacetime goods to wartime necessities and rationed materials needed for the war effort.
War Reparations	According to the Versailles Treaty, Germany was to pay several European nations for damage Germany caused during WWI. Because Germany could not pay these reparations, France occupied the Ruhr Valley, a German territory containing a wealth of natural resources. The Dawes Plan resolved the issue of debt repayment and occupation.
Warren Court	Term for the Supreme Court while Earl Warren was chief justice (1953-1969). This court was known for expanding civil rights, civil liberties, judicial power, and federal power. This angered conservatives.
Warsaw Pact	Treaty signed by the Soviet Union and satellite nations of eastern Europe. The treaty was created as a response to NATO and pledged assistance for mutual defense.
Wartime Economy	An economy that focuses on producing wartime goods rather than consumer goods.
Washington, Booker T.	Leader of the Tuskegee Institute. Advocated the education of African Americans so they could improve their economic state. Viewed as an accommodationist by other black leaders who wanted full equality.

Washington, George	Initiated the French and Indian War by confronting the French in the Ohio River Valley. Led the Continental Army to victory over the British during the Revolutionary War. Became the first president of the United States; he named the first cabinet and followed a strict foreign policy of isolationism.
Watergate Scandal	Scandal that took place during Nixon's presidency. The Committee to Re-elect the President (CRP) paid burglars to break into a Democratic office at the Watergate Hotel to photograph campaign documents and install listening devices. It was later found that Nixon had become aware of this but had kept it a secret. Impeachment proceedings were brought against Nixon; in response, he resigned from the presidency.
Watts Riot	A 6-day riot that took place in 1965 in the Los Angeles neighborhood of Watts when a black motorist was arrested on suspicion of drunk driving. During the arrest, a minor argument escalated into a fight. Angry at what they perceived as racist treatment by the police, the Watts community reacted in one of the most violent and destructive riots to take place in the 1960s. This signaled the end of nonviolent civil disobedience.
WAVES	The women's branch of the Navy during World War II. This allowed women to work in jobs men had held and released the men to fight in the war at sea.

Wealth Against Commonwealth	Book written by muckraker Henry Demarest Lloyd during the Progressive Era, illustrating the problems that arose due to monopolies.
Webster, Daniel	U.S. politician, most notably senator from Massachusetts.
Weld, Theodore Dwight	Abolitionist during the Reform Era who wrote *American Slavery As It Is*.
West African Squadron	Part of the British navy tasked with ensuring that no ships crossing the Atlantic Ocean were involved in the African slave trade. This caused the value of slaves in the United States to rise, which made slave owners even more opposed to abolition.
Whiskey Rebellion	Protest by farmers against the excise tax created by Hamilton during Washington's presidency. The farmers believed it was unlawful because they had not been represented. As it was so similar to direct taxes like the Stamp Tax, they felt their protest was continuing the spirit of the American Revolution. To end the protest, Washington rode with the army to the areas where the rebellion was strongest. The protests ended before the army even arrived. This illustrated that the Constitution, which allowed the federal government to tax and maintain an army, could be used to stop future rebellions.

Whitney, Eli	American inventor best known for inventing the cotton gin, which separated seeds from cotton, making cotton production (and therefore slavery) more profitable. Whitney also invented the concept of interchangeable parts, which was originally developed for the musket; it became invaluable in factories, as spare parts could be ahead of time, ensuring rapid repair of factory equipment.
Wilderness Campaign	Civil War battles instigated by General Grant, who realized that the Union had more troops and thus could sustain loss of life longer than the Confederacy. As a result, Grant initiated several battles and refused to retreat, even when the Union soldiers had massive casualties. Eventually, this strategy allowed him to defeat General Lee's Army of Northern Virginia.
Wilhelm, Kaiser	German emperor and King of Prussia. He supported Austria-Hungary during World War I.
Willard, Emma	Women's rights advocate who founded the first school that offered women higher education.
Williams, Roger	Puritan dissenter who lived in Massachusetts Bay. After advocating for a separation of church and state (which local officials viewed as "new and dangerous ideas"), he was exiled and established the new colony of Rhode Island.
Wilmot Proviso	Proposed by David Wilmot, this law would have forbidden slavery in all territories acquired in the Mexican Cession. The law was not passed and instead the Compromise of 1850 was instituted.

Wilson, Woodrow	President during the Progressive Era. He oversaw the creation of the Federal Reserve banking system and passed the Clayton Antitrust Act. Wilson believed in a foreign policy based on moral principles and was president during World War I. He created a peace plan to follow the war, which included the League of Nations.
Winthrop, Jonathan	The first governor of the Massachusetts Bay colony. He wanted the new colony to be "a city upon a hill," to serve as the model for all other religious communities.
Worchester v. Georgia	A Supreme Court case heard by the Marshall Court. It determined that the Cherokee Indians had the right to remain on their land, which had been established by a treaty with the U.S. government. Congress and Andrew Jackson did not respect this decision and passed the Indian Removal Act, which led to the Trail of Tears.
Works Progress Administration (WPA)	Job creation program established by the New Deal. It created jobs for unskilled men to construct public buildings and infrastructure projects.
World War I	A global war fought between the Allies and the Central Powers from 1914-1918. It began when Archduke Franz Ferdinand was assassinated by a Serbian nationalist organization. A system of secret alliances quickly made this issue between two nations a much larger conflict.

World War II	A global war that lasted from 1939-1945. The U.S. entered the war in 1941 after the Japanese attack at Pearl Harbor. The U.S. fought with the Allies against the Axis Powers. The Allies' victory stopped fascist regimes from expanding and also protected democracy.
Wounded Knee, Battle of	After forfeiting their lands to the U.S. government, the Plains Indians planned a religious ceremony known as the Ghost Dance to communicate with their dead ancestors and regain the land they had lost. The U.S. military was sent to maintain control; when a rifle discharged, confusion ensued, leading to indiscriminate shooting which left over 100 Indians and dozens of U.S. soldiers dead.
XYZ Affair	Confrontation between the U.S. and France. Began when U.S. diplomats went to meet with French foreign minister Charles-Maurice de Talleyrand to discuss ending the policy of France capturing U.S. ships. The diplomats were intercepted by three intermediaries who demanded a bribe of $250,000 to speak with Talleyrand. They refused to pay and returned to America. When the attempted bribery became known, Americans were outraged. Some, especially the warhawks who resided in the south and west, demanded a war. Instead, a period of unofficial fighting occurred between American and French ships in the Caribbean Sea. Eventually the fighting ended with the Convention of 1800.

Yalta Conference Meeting between the "Big Three," Franklin Roosevelt, Winston Churchill, and Joseph Stalin, to shape a post-war peace. Key parts of the agreement: Germany would be divided into four zones, Poland and other eastern European nations would be permitted to have free elections, and Russia would help defeat the Japanese in the Pacific when the war in Europe was finished.

Yellow Journalism A type of journalism that focuses very little on the facts and instead sensationalizes stories to increase a periodical's circulation. Practiced widely during the Gilded Age by William Randolph Hearst's and Joseph Pulitzer's newspapers. Contributed to the start of the Spanish-American War by swaying public opinion.

Yom Kippur War A war fought between a coalition of Arab nations and Israel. The war ended when a ceasefire was created by the United Nations. After the ceasefire, attempts to improve the relationship of Israel and its Arab neighbors were made, most notably the Camp David Accords.

Yorktown, Battle of Battle in which the Continental Army, assisted by the French, defeated the forces of British General Cornwallis. Although the war was not officially over, this was the last significant battle before the British were willing to grant the colonies their independence.

Zenger, Peter	Newspaper editor in the colony of New York. After his paper criticized royal governor William Cosby, Zenger was put on trial for libel. The jury found Zenger's derogatory statements against Cosby to be true and therefore not libelous. As a result, the jury supported the concept of freedom of the press in the colonies.
Zimmerman Telegram	A secret telegram sent from Germany to the government of Mexico during World War I. The telegram stated that if the U.S. went to war against Germany, then Mexico should attack the U.S. with the understanding that once the war was over and the U.S. was defeated, Mexico would regain control of land lost in the Mexican Cession. This message did not remain a secret, and when the U.S. government learned of this conspiracy, they declared war on Germany.

Made in the USA
Las Vegas, NV
09 March 2022

45334887R00075